Canada in the Atlantic Economy

CANADA IN THE ATLANTIC ECONOMY

Other studies to be published later in the series will deal with policies for the transitional period and problems of harmonizing customs practices, transport policies, etc. There will also be a summary study in which the implications of the more specialized studies will be drawn together in an assessment of the over-all impact of trade liberalization on the Canadian economy.

Transatlantic Economic Community:
Canadian Perspectives

H. Edward English

Published for the
Private Planning Association of Canada by University of Toronto Press

To William B. Lambert

These studies of "Canada in the Atlantic Economy" are dedicated with respect and gratitude to the late William B. Lambert, Chairman of the Board of the Private Planning Association of Canada from 1965 to 1967, who played a vital role in the development and supervision of the Atlantic Economic Studies Program, on which the publications are based.

His interest went far beyond his formal responsibility; he held a deep conviction concerning the importance of international cooperation among the North Atlantic nations. His untimely death came when the first draft studies had entered the early stages of publication.

© 1968 University of Toronto Press / Reprinted 2017
ISBN 978-1-4875-9837-2 (paper)

Foreword

There have been two outstanding developments in international trade policy during the past twenty years—the multilateral dismantling of trade barriers under the General Agreement on Tariffs and Trade, which has been the agency for several rounds of successful tariff negotiations since its inception in 1947, and the establishment of the European Economic Community and the European Free Trade Association in the late 1950s. In a period of reconstruction and then sustained growth, these policies have helped the participating nations of the Atlantic area to experience the benefits of international specialization and expanding trade. The wealth generated by trade and domestic prosperity has also made possible external aid programs to assist economic growth in the developing countries.

Whatever the trade and economic development problems of the future, it is widely acknowledged that the industrially advanced countries of the North Atlantic region must play an important role. It is also generally conceded that the ability of these countries to maintain their own economic growth and prosperity and to contribute to that of the less advanced nations will be greatly enhanced if they can reduce or remove the remaining trade barriers among themselves. Cooperation among Atlantic countries is now fostered by the GATT and by the Organisation for Economic Co-operation and Development. But the success of these and other approaches depends on the assessment by each country of the importance of international trade liberalization and policy coordination for its domestic economy and other national interests. This is particularly true for countries such as Canada which are heavily dependent upon export markets.

The Atlantic Economic Studies Program of the Private Planning Association of Canada was initiated to study the implications for Canada of trade liberalization and closer economic integration among the nations bordering the North Atlantic. It is planned to issue at least twelve paperbound volumes, incorporating over twenty studies by leading Canadian and foreign economists. Despite the technical nature of much of the subject matter, the studies have been written in language designed to appeal to the non-professional reader.

The directors and staff of the Private Planning Association wish to acknowledge the financial support which made this project possible—a grant from the Ford Foundation and the contributions of members of the Association. They are also appreciative of the help that has been provided by very many individuals in the preparation and review of all the studies— in discussions and correspondence with authors, at the Association's November, 1966, conference on "Canada and the Atlantic Economy," and on other occasions.

H. E. ENGLISH
Director of Research
Atlantic Economic Studies Program

Contents

1. Introduction

In recent years there have appeared many books and articles reviewing the course of Atlantic economic relations and endeavouring to prescribe for the future. The purpose of this brief book is not to re-examine or duplicate these efforts. Its more modest objective is twofold—first, to provide a basis for the analysis of the impact of a closer economic community among Atlantic countries upon the Canadian economy; and, second, to put forward a Canadian view (not *the* Canadian view) of the prospects for Atlantic community over the next few years. Something further needs to be said about these purposes so that what follows may be judged by appropriate criteria and with a reasonably explicit appreciation of the prejudices which may be involved.

Now that the formal internal barriers to trade in the two European free trade groupings are almost dismantled, Canada is the most important, almost the only, industrially advanced nation which is not now integrated in a market of at least a hundred million people, with the advantages of specialization and competitiveness which such integration implies. For this reason the further dismantling of trade barriers as a feature of an emerging Atlantic economic community, or on any comparable basis, would probably have more economic significance for Canada than for other countries of the North Atlantic region. For other countries, Atlantic community appears to have less economic meaning, precisely because they have already found a way to realize the kind of economic benefits of integration which might be derived for Canada from a far-reaching Atlantic economic grouping. It therefore becomes important not only that Canada should be aware of the economic implications of any substantial move toward the closer integration of Canada into the world economy, but also that the alternative vehicles for achieving this end be reviewed to determine their acceptability to other trading partners as well as their appropriateness for Canada.

There have been times, the last as recent as 1962, when Canada has missed the opportunity to help create a legal framework for trade negotiations which would have better suited Canadian purposes and which would be at least as effective and appropriate from the viewpoint of the United States and the other principal trading countries. No country with as great a stake in world trade as Canada's can afford to miss such opportunities to affect the kind of policy adopted in those world capitals where the main courses are charted. One way to ensure that such opportunities may be grasped in the future is through the systematic assessment of the most probable policies.

It must, in candour, be added that there have been few times in recent history when such an assessment would have been as difficult as it is now. The present Kennedy round of GATT negotiations has just been concluded, and the environment in which the main trading partners are operating is beset with doubts and difficulties: the great uncertainty affecting EFTA-EEC relations; the weakening of the military mainmast of the NATO vessel; the conflict of nationalism and federalism within the European Economic Community; the uncertainties and distractions introduced into Atlantic relationships by U.S.-China and USSR-China confrontations; and the increasing and almost overwhelming challenge of world economic development. Is the Atlantic community an outworn or irrelevant concept in this context? If not, what new form must it adopt to establish its relevance to these present challenges from within and without?

With reference to the second purpose of this paper, it should be emphasized that a Canadian view of North Atlantic relationships is likely to differ from those of an American or European in important ways. As already implied, it is much less political, though Canadian governments have always regarded the relationship with Britain as a balance wheel against too close integration and political identification with the United States. Canada's role on the world stage is conceived in ideal terms as "a leader of the middle powers," and perhaps, in particular, as a sympathetic listener and interpreter of the cause of economically developing and often politically uncommitted states in Africa and Asia. Canada has been reasonably active in world politics, but its own self-interest is not bound up in a political role as much as that of the United States, France, or Britain. While fundamentally North American in its outlook, Canada has never felt that preemptive sense of responsibility for the defence of the West which has understandably dominated the U.S. concept of NATO and, therefore, of the Atlantic community.

This is partly because Canadian attitudes toward Communism have differed somewhat from those of the United States. While private views run the full gamut from anathema to apologia, official views have tended to differ in at least two or three respects from those usually expressed in Washington. Canadians have not regarded Communism as monolithic:

they were never convinced of the view that the whole Communist world was run from Moscow, as leading U.S. spokesmen used to assert. In addition, Canadians have not been accepting U.S. strictures against trade with the Communist countries. They have questioned whether refusal to trade with a vast and well-endowed country, such as the Soviet Union, could be expected to improve the relative political and strategic position of the West. Canada's trade with China and Cuba has raised more serious doubts. While the China wheat deals may have been motivated primarily by self-interest, it is by no means clear that a refusal by Canada to make these deals would have improved the relative position of the West. Even with Cuba, a complete embargo has been politically possible only for military hardware, and then only in the context of a major confrontation. Finally, Canadian official opinions, like those of most European governments, have been less prone than Washington to regard any alternative to a Communist government as "democratic," and thus feel uncomfortable about the presumptuous application of the term "free world" to all non-Communist countries. All this said, Canadian governments have left no doubt that they share U.S. views on the propensity of the leading Communist governments to support military adventures and subversion and to recognize that massive U.S. power and the supporting system of alliances remain essential to contain attempts by Moscow or Peking to extend Communist control over other countries.

These Canadian views on the world's main contests are sketched out because they serve to identify particularly the differences between Canadian and U.S. attitudes. There are also important differences between Canadian and European attitudes. If Canadian governments have, at times, come closer to French or British attitudes toward Communism, they have also better understood American attitudes toward the developing world. They have recognized that, however unready some of the colonies were for political independence, the denial of independence was seldom likely to lead to the kind of guided and peaceful evolution which European governments favoured. Neither the maintenance of enlightened but unpopular "colonial" authority—as in Algeria—nor the sudden abandonment of colonial authority—as in the Belgian Congo—proved to be a guarantee against far-left regimes or utter political chaos.

Thus, Canada may be said to have less profound international political commitments and responsibilities than either the United States or the western Europeans. As a major exporting country, as a member of the Commonwealth, and as a neighbour of the United States, Canada's governments have been involved enough to be aware of the world's problems and of opportunities for a constructive role. Canada has responded to her opportunities to a commendable extent—considering that non-involvement might have been politically safer on occasion. But there have been enough instances of worthy performances—Suez and the Gaza strip, Cyprus, and so forth—that Canadians have developed a little smugness, a smugness which continues to cloak the rather more passive Canadian role of recent years.

It should be emphasized that underlying Canada's public positions on the main international issues lies a wide variety of attitudes, held with some complacency. Wheat deals apart, the day-to-day consensus for the bulk of the people, even in such an open economy as Canada's, is not concerned with the world's main conflicts. All one needs to do to confirm this is to note which views get the most prominent treatment in the average run of Canadian newspapers, which political views receive front-page attention, which publications are most widely purchased, which topics most attract the interest of broadcasters. The only international topic which regularly receives prominent attention is the love-hate relationship with the United States. Even this is apparently received with a blandness which frustrates those who would like to make more political capital out of it and obscures the conscientious efforts of private groups and public servants to solve particular problems of Canadian-American relations with sense and maturity. At the very least, the variety in Canadian opinion itself may serve to increase the scope for Canadian foreign policy, while the general complacency of a prosperous society serves to ensure that when the government pleases one group by an action in the international sphere, it greatly offends no one else.

Regional Canadian attitudes bear some examination in this context, in part because they are changing. Because of wheat, the prairie attitude has always been the most internationalist—a fact again reflected in the strong internationalist economic positions adopted at the Western Conference of the Liberal party in August, 1966. But whereas western Canadians were formerly oriented to European, especially U.K., markets, their market outlook is now much broader and includes Japan, China, and Russia for wheat, and Japan and the United States for minerals now produced throughout western Canada. Furthermore, the role of the United States and other foreign capital in the development of prairie oil and potash, together with some of the recent developments in British Columbia's forest products, has made western Canada very sceptical indeed about anti-foreign-investment attitudes.

At the other end of the country, the Atlantic provinces remain outward-looking, with market interests in Europe and the United States. It has been in central Canada that nationalist economic interests have historically been strongest, though these areas have also contributed much to Canada's exports of pulp and paper and non-ferrous metals. Both Quebec and Ontario have in the past experienced fundamental conflict between resource industries and secondary manufacturing, with the former aligning themselves with export industries in other parts of the country, and the manufacturers, dependent almost exclusively on the domestic Canadian market, clinging to protection. In the postwar years, and especially in the last four years, Canadian manufacturers have been changing their attitude. Although they never expect to be so heavily export-oriented as the industries based on Canada's natural resources, they now recognize that they have an opportunity for specialized production, competitive in many lines with manufacturers in the markets of the U.S. Midwest. One indication that the political climate concerning trade policy in Ontario has changed is that the Ontario minister of trade and industry has become one of the strongest advocates of freer trade in manufactures with the United States. Those who show less confidence in their ability to compete are mainly among the small manufacturers and particularly among family firms: many international companies with Canadian or foreign head offices consider themselves capable of competing internationally.

In Quebec, a similar change is occurring. Though the resource industries have always been predominant in Quebec, changes in attitude are occurring in the paper, chemicals, and machinery and equipment industries, for example, which parallel the changes in Ontario and which bring the views of these manufacturers closer to those of the resource industries.

Political attitudes arising out of Canada's cultural diversity are sometimes cited as affecting Canada's international policies—a French-Canadian affinity for France and a strong attachment, especially in Ontario and the Atlantic provinces, to Britain. In fact, there is little evidence that these sentiments exert much influence on Canada's international trade policies and on attitudes toward them. They tend only to reinforce national sentiments which support Canada's overseas associations as a counterbalance to the close relationship, both economic and political, with the United States. It is a fundamental feature of Canada's political stance to seek national identity by a delicate balance among its international relationships, rather than to reject such associations for a purely continental solution or a protected nationalism.

The question to which attention must now be directed is this: is the prospect of a developing Atlantic community sufficiently strong to provide a principal vehicle through which Canada's economic needs and political interests can be served? The answer to this ultimately depends not on Canada's power or initiative, but on the intrinsic merits for Canada of integration with such an extensive grouping of nations and on whether the net political and economic benefits are substantial enough to command support for such a community among the principal North Atlantic countries.

Definition of the Atlantic economic community

The concept of "Atlantic community" is vague. It is favoured by people of varying interests—from idealists such as Clarence Streit, who views it as a federal union of European and North American peoples, to "hard-nosed" military men who are almost exclusively concerned with the maintenance of the NATO alliance against Communist aggression. By many others it is thought to be an extension of the European Economic Community, enlarged by membership of some or all of the countries of the European Free Trade Area, to include the United States and Canada.

It may be useful from the outset to draw the distinction employed by Professor Balassa between integration and cooperation. Integration refers to a long-term commitment to remove the barriers obstructing flows of goods and resources, whereas cooperation usually means only agreement on a system of rules by which the parties are willing to abide, to stabilize and improve their economic or other relationships. The boundary is indistinct, but the leading institutions of the present day can be classified fairly readily. The Organisation for Economic Co-operation and Development is clearly a body for promoting voluntary cooperation. Its work includes the study of economic conditions in member countries, the search for a consensus of views and of advice on stabilization and growth policies among advanced countries, and consultation on development aid. It can be the informational and consultative base for Atlantic economic community. Its work is coordinated with that of the International Monetary Fund through Working Party 3, which is a closely parallel organization to the "Group of Ten" founded by the Fund to study national balance of payments situations and their effect on international monetary equilibrium and to discuss measures for international monetary reform. There is no similar overlapping of institutions between OECD and GATT; but to the extent that OECD consultation bears on trade policy, there is very little likelihood of conflict.

NATO goes beyond cooperation and provides for integrated defence. This integration has involved so dominant a U.S. role that NATO is now considered obsolete as a basis for true community, quite apart from the implications of Gaullist nationalism.

An Atlantic economic community will be defined as an arrangement requiring explicit commitment to integration of the economies of the principal states of the North Atlantic region. This definition would imply a treaty arrangement embodying (at least) a substantial reduction of trade barriers and agreement to avoid national policies which discriminate against imports or subsidize exports and thus frustrate the purpose of reducing obstacles to trade. It might go beyond this to provide for free movement of factors of production and explicit forms of coordination of transport policies. This definition covers anything from a "low-tariff club" through a free trade area and customs union to a full economic union.

The principal question which is begged by the concept of economic community is membership. How small can it be and still be worthwhile? How big should it be to achieve the greatest benefits? To answer these questions it is necessary to adopt an assumption about alternatives. For example, if one were to compare the implications of universal free trade with those of North Atlantic integration, the latter would usually be rejected on economic grounds. The discussion of Atlantic community must be based on two premises: that it may be easier to achieve integration on a narrower base than on a universal base; and that economic cooperation and integration on a wider scale may be promoted by the successes of the smaller group. The formation of the present European communities was based in the first premise and was accepted by other countries because of a tentative acceptance of the second premise, though its validity is still being tested in GATT, in EFTA-EEC relations, in efforts toward Atlantic economic community, and in the development of the Associated Overseas Territories.

The minimum membership which could justify the name Atlantic Economic Community would incorporate the United States and at least one of the two European communities. Under these limited circumstances, the membership would have to be open to other countries on non-restrictive terms, otherwise it would be more likely to warrant criticism on the grounds that it might perpetuate the division in Europe and would be identified as a white man's or a rich man's club. On the other hand, a relatively small group of like-minded nations could improve their bargaining position vis-à-vis those countries which are satisfied with narrower horizons and could initiate a gradual movement toward economic integration among all industrially advanced states, including Japan, Australia, and New Zealand, as well as those in North America and western Europe. The "dynamics" of the institutional forms which embody an idea such as Atlantic economic community are, like all social dynamics, difficult to assess in advance. Statesmanship may, nevertheless, be based on the courage to act on just such assessments. For such an act is the name of Robert Schuman revered.

To be judged a success, any form of Atlantic economic community should accommodate four criteria:

1. It should preserve the present degree of integration in western Europe and not deter any further integration which is compatible with the satisfaction of the other three criteria.

2. It should provide a basis for strengthening prospects for the integration of, and cooperation among, economically advanced nations with market economies. The satisfaction of this criterion depends primarily on the willingness of two countries—the United States and Japan—to participate. An important special aspect of this criterion is cooperation in perfecting international monetary arrangements—for which this group of countries has a special responsibility.

3. It should contribute as much as possible to the establishment of economically sound flows of East-West trade within Europe and to the economic bases of coexistence between the developed members of the Communist and non-Communist groups.

4. It should provide a basis for the most effective possible contribution to the development of the less economically advanced countries of Africa, Asia, and South America. The work of the DAC of the OECD reflects acceptance of the principle that joint action by the advanced countries is desirable, *if not essential*, to ensure the most effective economic aid program. The demands of the developing countries, put forward in connection with the first UNCTAD in 1964, challenge the North Atlantic countries (and Japan) to find a common trade policy program to meet the needs, if not all the demands, of the less developed three-quarters of this planet.

These far-reaching criteria suggest that North Atlantic economic community can be an end in itself only in a very limited sense. Rather it is a technique for meeting urgent needs of the world economy—needs which are probably more urgent than the effective functioning of the North Atlantic economic or political community itself. An appropriate form of Atlantic community may be the best, or the only, means of meeting the greater challenges on which world peace and stability will depend for the rest of this century.

2. Europe in Search of Consensus

Although it is reasonably easy to delineate the criteria by which the role of an Atlantic economic community may be judged, once one begins to analyze the problems which will affect the future peace and prosperity of the North Atlantic area, the lines are very difficult to draw. The unity and evolution of the EEC depend on the resolution of differences in attitudes among its members to Britain and the United States. The future of EFTA depends on attitudes toward unity in the EEC on the one hand and on the possibility of Atlantic economic groupings on the other. The relationship with eastern Europe depends on both EEC and U.S. attitudes and, in turn, will determine whether and when German unification is likely to occur. And, of course, the possibility of concessions on matters which affect relations between North America and Europe will determine whether agreement can be achieved on international monetary policy and world development policy.

In view of these interrelationships, the following discussion will be divided into three chapters. Chapter 2 will cover two topics: (*a*) integration in western Europe—EEC and EFTA; and (*b*) East-West relations —trade and German reunification. Chapter 3, "North America and Europe: Cooperation or Coexistence," will focus on the role of NATO and the prospects for economic community. Chapter 4, "A World Economic Role for Atlantica?," will deal with the economic role of North America and Europe in the world, treating (*a*) monetary stabilization and (*b*) strategy for economic development, covering supply of capital and access to markets. Chapter 5 will deal with "Canada's Choice"—a review of the range of choices available to Canada and Canada's probable policy preferences, given alternative assumptions about competitive potential and national goals.

EEC and EFTA

Integration is the magic word. How much integration is likely and desirable in Europe, and indeed in the world? For many years, the question has not been put in this way because the foreign policy viewpoints of the principal powers assumed that integration was the key to peace in Europe. Ironically, some of the same policy-makers, especially in Washington, often seemed to assume that disintegration was the key to peace in Africa and Asia. This contrast is, in fact, only a reflection of the need, which is always present in international relations, to balance desirability and likelihood. The reluctance of developing countries to enter customs unions with other similar countries is perhaps an illustration of the rejection of the economic (and political) benefits of integration in the interest of enjoying the political fruits of self-determination. The path to appreciation of the limitations on political choice lies by way of one or more missed economic opportunities.

How and why is integration desirable? The answer is in part economic, in part political. Among the familiar economic benefits of integration are its contribution to trade creation through improved economic efficiency and resultant economic growth and its use to ensure the relative economic strength of the participating countries, largely through trade diversion. Among the most crucial considerations are the sizes and attitudes of the integrating countries. In general, the larger the integrating group, the more the trade-creating effect. However, any important group of countries may divert trade. Whether they choose to do so depends on their political attitudes towards the "outsiders," and also to some extent on their political philosophy. The more *dirigiste* their attitude, the more probable that external tariffs will remain high. On the other hand, governments can be less interventionist the more effectively this market system can be made to work; and the freeing of international trade provides a meaningful alternative to more interventionist means of improving the structural efficiency and competitiveness of industry. Economic stabilization policy is less constrained under these circumstances, since a sizable group of countries must be less dependent upon external trade and the possible origins of economic cycles in fluctuating exports. This calls attention to the great strength of economic groupings. They have tended to come into existence because the member countries are prepared to commit themselves within the group to a degree of policy coordination which they would not risk on a more multilateral basis. The danger of a limited group arises out of the possibility that much can be won from the rest of the world through discrimination. This danger will be minimized if those outside the area can counteract the benefits of discrimination.

Integration is also politically desirable, as a means of achieving world peace, because it reduces the possibility of war in at least two ways. First, through economic integration countries lose the means of independent action. Only those countries with vast and diversified production capacity can sacrifice integration without weakening their ability to "go it alone" in military adventures. Fortunately, for the same basic reasons, such countries have the least motive for expansion and the most to lose economically, especially given the nature of modern war.

Secondly, through integration political power is dispersed. To a considerable extent this is related to the effect of increased economic integration, but it goes beyond. Integration makes it less possible for one or two economic or social groups to exercise a dominant political influence within a country. In its extreme forms this proposition is easy to defend. Geographically large and diversified countries have not only a varied industry structure but also a regional specialization which makes it very difficult for one or two groups to concentrate power in their hands. The consequence in such circumstances is that federalism is often adopted, and this institutionalizes the dispersion of power.

For smaller countries, one cannot so easily generalize about the net effect of integration. On the one hand, such countries are able to specialize more effectively as foreign markets become accessible. On the other hand, the fuller realizing of a nation's economic potential permits industrialization based in part on exports of those processed goods for which its pattern of natural and human resources gives it a comparative advantage, and in part on the greater income generated by integration in the domestic market. If the comparative advantages a country enjoys are strongly in the line of agricultural or other natural products, freer trade may possibly result in more specialization, and thus in more concentration of economic and political power. Some of the smaller tropical developing countries may fit this description, but for most natural tropical products trade barriers are already low or non-existent.

For more industrially advanced countries, the implications of economic integration are dominated by the more complex effects of industrialization.[1] In western Europe, historical and present-day moves toward economic integration have produced no instance of more concentrated economic power and at least a plausible case for the opposite tendency. In nineteenth-century Britain, the effect of freer trade was to strengthen the position of industrial management and labour, but agricultural interests continued to play an important role in British social and political life, and the variety of interests reflected in the structure of industry and in the labour movement

---

[1]Some authors place emphasis upon the possibility that integration and resultant specialization may mean a higher per capita income but that aggregate income might even fall as a result of a possible loss of population if mobility is permitted. Both the application of the law of comparative advantage, with modification of its less realistic assumptions (regarding transport cost and constant productivity), and empirical observation suggest that this is a very special case.

and distribution trades has resulted in political parties which depend for their success on a broad "compromise" appeal to the various social and economic groups. The effect of trade liberalization in the European Economic Community has been to shift product patterns within industries or individual firms rather than to obliterate whole industries. Perhaps the one effect arising out of economic integration which is reasonably uniform is the common concern of economic groups to assure continuity of the benefits. Both the French farmer and the *patronat*, having adapted to the challenges and opportunities of the Common Market, were disturbed by the political disagreements which threatened the progress of the Community in the last half of 1965.

To return to the theme with which this discussion began, integration can have beneficial effects, both economic and political. Furthermore, these effects are broadly recognized by industrially advanced countries and especially by those bordering the North Atlantic. However, each national government measures these benefits against the advantages of nationalistic policies and sometimes decides in favour of the latter. Sometimes these decisions rest only on short-term political advantage, sometimes on more sophisticated appraisals of long-term national advantage. For a government facing electoral challenges every two to four years, it may appear costless to succumb to the temptation to rely on an emotional appeal to that omnipresent xenophobia by which individuals salve their frustrations and by which political and social groups jockey for prestige and power. Such a choice seemed costless indeed in the days before the wars of the twentieth century, but democracy at its demagogic worst has subsequently made its contribution to the conditions of international conflict. However, more fundamentally, the value of nationalistic policy postures has seemed to vary directly with the size of nations and their anticipations of achieving a future leadership role and inversely with their past experience of the cost of international conflict (discounted for the number of years since the last war).

In Europe the smaller countries on all counts place a low value on nationalism and tend to favour integration on as wide a scale as possible, incorporating at least all non-Communist Europe but if possible extending to the whole Atlantic area. Some of them, like the Netherlands and Denmark, are so heavily dependent on international trade and so enmeshed geographically and otherwise with the greater powers that they place all their stakes on the sublimation of nationalism. Others, like Sweden and Switzerland, have chosen to depart only slightly from the same course, and then because formal neutrality has paid dividends in the past, while for Austria and Finland, neutralization has been a condition of cold war equilibrium. Even Italy has thrown in its lot with those who have no illusions concerning the lessons of the past and no pretensions to grandeur through nationalism. Among the nations of western Europe, only Germany, the United Kingdom, and France remain in ambiguous positions. The suspicion of a German reversion to nationalism arises more out of her neighbours' remembrance of past sins than out of evidence of present propensities in this direction. So long as West Germany's role is confined to its significant part in the internal affairs of western Europe, it seems likely to be motivated by her economic interest in the development of the European Economic Community. The only important vestiges of economic nationalism for West Germany lie in the delaying action fought on behalf of agriculture in recognition of domestic political realities. The question of German unification also raises concern about possible resurgence of German nationalism, but this depends on initiatives taken by others, especially France, the Soviet Union, and the United States. These will be reviewed later.

For Britain, like Germany and France, size and economic potential still tempt the government to seek a role in European leadership. But as the only undefeated member of the three, Britain sought, at least in the early postwar years, to play a wider role, one which arose out of her senior partnership in the Commonwealth and special wartime association with the United States. She rejected commitments to integrate in European economic and defence arrangements out of a mixture of the nationalism of victory and involvement in post-imperial economic and political commitments. Then, when it was too late, she moved to the industrial free trade area concept by which a European commitment could have been added without abandonment of other obligations or sacrifice of other opportunities. And finally in 1961, Britain applied for membership in EEC, quite explicitly opting for a leadership role in Europe as the most promising context in which to maintain a role in world politics. Furthermore, Britain's continuing economic problems seem to point toward such a bold measure as participation in the EEC. The need for dismantling of trade barriers so that "fresh winds of competition" could blow on the more lethargic and comfort-oriented sectors of British industry and the opportunity for a wider role for the London capital markets once Britain was an integrated part of an enlarged European community—these are the economic ingredients of the case for British entry. It should be added that membership in the EEC is not the only means by which Britain's economic potential could be better realized. Any substantial trade arrangement which would help to restore Britain's competitive strength would do as well and could thus augment Britain's political, as well as economic, role. The economic advantage of the European idea is mainly that it looked, and perhaps still looks, like the most feasible prospect. Equivalent regional arrangements would depend upon the United States, which has evidenced no official interest in such an approach, and substantial economic integration by the multilateral route depends on a further exchange of concessions between the EEC and the United States—and that is improbable on present evidence.

France has experienced a rebirth of national spirit, and with it a return to some traditional attitudes on France's role in Europe and the world. Favouring this tradition are France's high degree of economic self-sufficiency (higher than for other countries of similar size) and the prosperity which has made it possible for France to afford the space and military hardware which marks the first order of nationhood, at least among many contemporary political leaders. But above all, France has achieved stable government and a leadership which symbolizes the continuity of French independence even through defeat. After ten years of de Gaulle, it is not surprising that more emphasis is placed upon the role of leadership than on the circumstances which made it possible to rebuild— the Marshall Plan, cooperative reconstruction leading to the founding of the EEC, and the unilateral devaluation of 1958, which combined effectively with the dismantling of trade barriers to enable French agriculture and industry to develop confidently on the basis of new export opportunities and import challenges. One wonders whether the EEC will permit Britain the same *combination* of exchange adjustment and trade liberalization if on other counts the terms of admission are some day agreed. The fact that the economic foundations of modern France were well established by 1958, through the efforts of a series of economically sophisticated leaders such as Schuman and Pinay, is clearly undervalued by Gaullists. President de Gaulle has made one great contribution to France's restoration—he ended the Algerian conflict. It is a supreme irony that he was brought to power to maintain the Algerian departments but that he will probably be praised mostly by historians as the man who recognized the unreality of the attempt. Like successive British leaders of the postwar period, he was one of the few continental leaders who recognized that the issue in Africa could no longer be whether the Africans were ready to govern themselves through political institutions modeled on Westminster or the Chambre des Deputés, but rather how to ensure that the risk of local tyranny or takeover by other European powers could be minimized during the many years which would be necessary to evolve stable and reasonably democratic governments. The greatest immediate effect of the end of the Algerian war, however, was on France itself. Political sores which were expected to fester for a generation healed overnight. French resources and energies could be turned to other more promising objectives, such as an improved standard of living. However, de Gaulle chose to divert a substantial share of these resources and energies to the symbols and substance of a new nationalism, which could prove to be as great and as dangerous an illusion as the preservation of colonialism.

Gaullism has implications at several levels—within non-Communist Europe, for NATO and other relations with the United States, in East-West relations, and even for policies affecting the developing countries. Only the first two of these will be discussed in this chapter. Although the EEC has passed into the third and final stage of transition to the formation of the full customs union, this was accomplished to a large extent by masking the implications of rule by majority rather than unanimity, and it is clear that, if on any issue one of the three larger powers were in danger of being outvoted, the EEC would enter a new crisis. The crisis of 1965 has raised doubt about the possibility of extending the power of the Commission, and particularly about the development of an association between the Brussels technocracy and a parliament of Europe, whether that at Strasbourg or any other. When de Gaulle has passed from the scene, many "Europeans" expect that political evolution will again be evident. But may not new forms arise? To extend the evolution analogy, is the "creature" called Europe the fittest to survive? The circumstances of the 1950s are unlikely to recur, and those of the late 1960s and 1970s may favour another course of institutional development. Even within the Community there are at least two factors which could force it to change its form: (*a*) the German interest in reunification or possibly in a revival of nationalism in response to French nationalism; (*b*) the possibility that future French (or other EEC) leaders will stress the role of the EEC Council of Ministers rather than that of the Elysée Palace in devising a common European economic policy, thus at one and the same time removing the objectionable feature of the de Gaulle position which so obviously intends a dominant role for France, curbing the scope of Commission activities and deliberately obviating the evolution of parliamentary institutions.

This last possibility might be further stressed because it could well appeal to Britain, to whom national identity is also important. The position of Britain may continue in doubt for some time. For de Gaulle, there is little advantage to actually permitting British admission to the EEC, though there is every reason for keeping her just offshore by indications of interest sufficiently strong and frequent to keep the British Isles from drifting further out into the Atlantic. Even if present efforts fail, there might be a new round of negotiations after de Gaulle's departure unless Britain has been forced to turn to a new course. Those Commission "Eurocrats" who already regard Britain with suspicion might fear further delays in the evolution of supranational institutions. On the other hand, they may by that time be reconciled to a new, less ambitious pace of development toward European political unity. Under these circumstances, the effect of Britain's membership on the roles now played by France and Germany would determine the prospect and terms of her membership. Given the domination of EEC affairs by France, British entry would be bound to dilute this position, and France would therefore become enthusiastic only if there were compensatory gains from Britain's participation. To anticipate the later discussion, it seems clear that such gains would arise only if Britain's membership in the EEC were to improve the bargaining position of western Europe vis-à-vis the two superpowers.

But even though this may provide a very real motivation bringing EFTA and EEC together, the terms are likely to be much more favourable for Britain if her economic strength is restored. Much has been written about Britain's economic position, and it would be a bold analyst who would claim to be able to diagnose the British problem in a few words or paragraphs. For the purposes of this paper it may be sufficient to note what is common to most diagnoses, that the British economy is not in permanent general decline, but that its weaknesses relate to uncompetitiveness and inadequate productivity and perhaps to certain international commitments which it could slough off if it would. Furthermore, it is usually agreed that unilateral or reciprocal removal of trade barriers would contribute much to Britain's competitiveness and that other domestic measures and even devaluation are likely to work effectively to improve Britain's international position only if they are accompanied by closer integration of Britain into an international grouping of countries which includes industrial powers capable of challenging British industry in the domestic market and providing a market for a wide range of British manufactured specialties. Britain needs to explore ways of better exploiting its opportunities within EFTA and through multilateral efforts and new regional groups, as well as through a renewed effort to join the EEC. If some of these opportunities could have been explored before the recent application to Brussels, it might have improved Britain's bargaining position. The crucial issue which seems likely to delay the renewed negotiations is Britain's financial position. Ironically, one of Britain's principal contributions to the Community could be the experience and prestige of the financial institutions of the City, which could provide the institutional core of a European capital market. However, this cannot occur so long as Britain's economic position is not such as to ensure confidence in the pound. The French government has hinted at its reluctance to accept Britain as a member of EEC while her financial position remains insecure, an attitude which lends itself to cynical interpretation in the light of the role which membership in the EEC is intended to play in restoring British strength and removing the uncertainties now affecting both industrial planning and growth policy.

One may therefore conclude that the course of integration in western Europe, having been interrupted by the Gaullist hiatus, may not take on quite the same character again. The familiar bottle (or bottles) will remain, but may be filled with new wine, lacking the heady flavour of the first postwar decade but of a strength and stability sufficient, it may be hoped, to generate lasting quality and not to degenerate again into the vinegar of traditional nationalism. To a degree as yet uncomprehended, the prospect of a good vintage may rest with nations and events outside western Europe, and it is to the relationship of Europe to these countries that we now turn.

East-West relations

One of the great changes in the 1960s is the change in circumstances governing East-West relations. Western Europe has always suffered from schizophrenia in its dealings with the East: on the one hand there has been the hankering after the trade and cultural relationships of the past and on the other the overwhelming fear of aggression and subversion. Many Western leaders have based their domestic political power on an anti-Communist front. In the case of Germany there has been the added temptation to find a basis for reunification.

The principal changes in recent years have emerged in part from the success of NATO and of European integration, and the greater consequent strength of the West in dealing with the Soviet Union and its satellites. In part they have also risen out of the schisms—the China-USSR conflict in the East and the France-U.S. dispute in the West. The USSR has become more conservative both as the result of its economic prosperity and because peaceful coexistence with the West makes it easier to ensure the support of the other eastern Europeans in the quarrel with China. For France, the moderating position of the European Communist governments makes it easier to contemplate measures compatible with de Gaulle's concept of a Europe extending from the Atlantic to the Urals. Furthermore, given the uncertainty of Franco-German relations after the retirement of Adenauer, the possibility of French deals with the East helps to ensure Bonn's attentiveness to French interests. The present government of Germany continues to view with mixed feelings any possibility of a deal combining reunification and disarmament, though Brandt as foreign minister seems less disturbed by this possibility.

Again it is impossible to define fully the relevant circumstances without reference to transatlantic relations. The United States is likely to continue to discourage the German government from contemplating any reunification deal acceptable to the Soviet Union. In short, political changes in East-West relations involving anything as important as a change in the military role of West Germany are unlikely to occur unless there is an estrangement between western Europe and the United States. It is possible that further aggravation of U.S.-China relations may encourage Europeans to search for a common middle ground which could be appealing not only to France but to more and more people in Germany and Britain as well. However, the governments of these countries will resist anything which would further disrupt NATO, so long as it is possible to maintain a non-involvement position in Indo-China, and the Soviet Union and France can do very little except generate embarrassing propaganda about U.S. policy unless Germany, at least, is willing to give up its close association with the United States.[2]

Trade is another matter. There is already a substantial volume of trade between East and West Germany and the scope of expanding trade with the East generally is growing with the productive power of the Communist countries and the decentralization of their foreign trade policies. Trade between eastern and western Europe tripled in the decade from 1953 to 1963 and the Communist share of western Europe's imports rose by one-third, though it was still less than 5 percent of the total imports of the area.

There is little left of the rather curious attitude that trade with the East would have significant adverse strategic implications for the West, and even the United States seems anxious to find a way of expanding trade, if the constraints imposed by its shipping and other interests can somehow be removed or evaded. Historically, exports from the East have been primarily foodstuffs and industrial raw materials and the imports have been primarily manufactures. While the East has been a net importer of bulk foodstuffs in more recent years, it has shown a capacity at times to export forest products, non-ferrous metals, and oil. The large unit scale of new production facilities in these industries and the possibility of large-scale errors in planning have introduced the danger of instability in trade flows. During the postwar period, the Soviet Union has increased its share of Western markets for softwood lumber and experienced occasional jumps in exports of aluminum and oil, but these developments have not dominated the long-term changes in market patterns. On the continent of Europe, these have been dominated by the effect of the formation of the free-trade groupings.

2Among the most important books on the future of East-West relations in Europe is Zbigniew Brzezinski's *Alternative to Partition*, New York, McGraw-Hill, 1965.

There are certain risks in the future of East-West trade. If the Soviet Union requires imports of capital goods, it may at times be tempted to divert food and raw material to the export markets to obtain the supplies of foreign exchange required. Students of the Soviet economy have pointed out that its accounting methods tend to favour raw material exports.[3] Producers in the West have shown considerable interest in avoiding what they regard as a potentially very troublesome and almost uncontrollable form of dumping. However, there are grounds for reassurance. The Soviet Union is increasingly recognizing that its capacity to trade will depend on normalizing trade flows and that there are substantial exchange costs in massive dumping. Perhaps most important, the recognition of the advantages of introducing more decentralized management of production and distribution is likely to result in a more economic system of pricing.

The question of competitive granting of credits to Communist countries has caused disagreement among Western countries. The United States has generally opposed longer-term credits on the grounds that these are a form of aid and that aid should be reserved for those who need it most. Others point out that all credit is aid, that there is little difference between "long-term" credit and short-term credits which are renewed, and that the Communists are as good credit risks as alternative buyers. Furthermore, if failure to grant credit induced uneconomic trading policies on the part of the Communists, European production and trade patterns could be adversely affected. Of course, in this instance, the restriction of credit might add a further inducement to produce and sell gold. Whether this makes a positive contribution to the allocation of productive resources or even an appropriate supplement to monetary reserves is too complex a question for this paper, given its marginal relevance to our topic.

For many of the eastern European countries there are indications of improved prospects for exchange of manufactures, and it seems most probable that East-West trade can be developed in these, as well as in the raw materials already mentioned. However, spectacular growth in the relative importance of this trade will be limited by the continuing complexities of trade between partners with different forms of economic organization and different patterns of consumer taste arising out of a marked gap between living standards. Although trade may make some contribution to closer cooperation between the East and West, it should not in itself be important enough to affect political relationships in western Europe.

The influence of the United States on European economic affairs is vastly more important and may yet hold the secret of both economic and political

---

[3]Ian M. Drummond, *Canada's Trade with the Communist Countries of Eastern Europe*, Montreal, Canadian Trade Committee, 1966, chap. II.

trends in Europe over the coming decade. The possibility of greatly increased Soviet prestige and influence in western Europe appears to rest not on Soviet policy nor indeed on de Gaulle or any prospective French or western European leader, but as always upon the danger of error or diplomatic default. Though the game in the 1960s and 1970s has changed, the trump cards remain in the same hands.

3. North America and Europe: Cooperation or Coexistence?

The role of the United States in Europe since 1945 has been described so often that no reiteration is necessary. The financial support for reconstruction; the encouragement of European cooperation and integration; the shield of NATO which reassured the private investor and government planner—all these contributed greatly to the European miracle. But the whole postwar relationship between Europe and the United States was a transitional one. In the longer sweep of history it may be regarded as one of two twentieth-century transitions in the Atlantic area. The longer and earlier period, beginning slowly toward the end of the First World War and ending during the Second, saw the entry of the United States into world affairs as an active participant. Before the First World War the independent imperial states of Europe outweighed the United States. By midway in the Second World War, U.S. power and wealth outstripped that of all Europe west of the Soviet border. But with the greater destructive effects of the war upon Europe, the pendulum of power and wealth had swung past its equilibrium and a new transition became necessary—a period during which the economic position of western Europe would again be restored relative to that of the United States.

The postwar equilibrium would have entirely new determinants and characteristics. Of these the two most important were the rise of Soviet Communism and the end of colonialism. The effect of Soviet power was to make the problem of reconstruction more urgent and to encourage the cooperative approach to its solutions. It is now becoming safe to admit publicly what an important role Stalin played in the miracle of European recovery.

The end of colonialism ensured that the relative position of western Europe would never be quite the same again, though the economic loss arising from the decline of colonialism should not be overestimated. It was the disposal of investments necessitated by the war, and not the liberation of the colonies, that most reduced the economic value of the imperial systems. The postwar growth records show that, in spite of any trade losses which might be attributable to the change in colonial status, the growth of western Europe has far outstripped that of most of the former colonies and of less developed countries generally.

Perhaps the unifying theme should, after all, be the technological revolution, with its particular implications for transport and communications. On the one hand, it is this which has enabled the realization of so much of the economic potential of the United States and the Soviet Union, the countries of continental size and proportions. On the other hand, in its communications manifestations, it made the colonial system obsolete and made the social and economic lags irrelevant to political self-determination.

The great transitions in Atlantic relations are over, or nearly so, but the conditions of the equilibrium are still unclear. The system of equations by which a stable relationship between Europe and America will be defined, if at all, contains at least one equation defining the Soviet role in Europe, a number of others for the various groups of developing countries, and possibly a special one for China.

The question may be raised, why dwell so much upon the North Atlantic relationship in a world in which the great issues may lie to the east and south of this favoured area? The answer may be "why, indeed?" But if a focus on the North Atlantic has any significance, it must arise out of a conviction that the appropriate relationship between the advanced industrial countries which share liberal political aspirations may be the essential condition, or at least the most favourable foundation, for world peace and the achievement of an adequate standard of economic welfare.

What can be learned from the successes and failures of the postwar period now ending, and from the new thinking which has now begun, about the nature and effectiveness of the Atlantic community that is likely to emerge? It is now not the great successes of the period that deserve most attention, but rather the failures, the experiences that reveal the problems which still face those who would promote closer cooperation and economic integration. Each of the three leading Western countries—Britain, France, and the United States—has contributed to the sense of disunity.

Britain's contribution was the product of victory. As the only western European country which did not suffer defeat, the United Kingdom entered the reconstruction era in a euphoric state regarding her prospective national role in the postwar world. The special relation between Britain and the United States was nourished by the respect in which both Churchill and Bevin were held in Washington. The challenges and frustrations of austerity did not call for resolution in a European context because the continental countries were worse off than Britain and continued to be so until well into the 1950s. At the time when the will to end Franco-German conflict and the need for economic recovery compelled the six continental countries to form the European Coal and Steel Community and to try to organize a European defence community, Britain did not foresee the compelling argument for participation. To be a leader in the Europe of the early 1950s was not an attractive alternative to the transatlantic and Commonwealth role, particularly if it took a form which might eventually compromise Britain's other relationships. Nevertheless, Britain missed an opportunity and left a legacy of doubt on the continent as to Britain's real interest in integration. Ironically, by the time she recognized the desirability of some explicit involvement in European economic integration, in 1956, it proved to be just too late, though if it had not been for the rise of de Gaulle, the industrial free trade area might have come into being.

The contribution of France to the world's current problems was her mixed record in managing the decolonization process. It was apparently difficult for the weak governments of the Fourth Republic to face the reality that Africans and Asians preferred self-government to continued participation in the French cultural and political community. The French defeat in Indo-China left lasting scars in France itself and a legacy of civil war in southeast Asia. Only the compensating political illusions and economic realities of the de Gaulle era were sufficient to make possible a resolution of the Algerian conflict. Had it not been for that conflict, there is little doubt that the Fourth Republic would have survived. Its economic policies, and particularly the combined effect of commitment to EEC membership and the devaluation of 1958, would have assured economic prosperity. Indeed, except for the economic drain caused by the Algerian war, France might have been better off, since without de Gaulle it would not have become committed to the expensive luxury of an independent nuclear deterrent and other high-priced military and space equipment. However essential de Gaulle may have been to the resolution of France's imperial problem, it is highly probable that without him events in Europe would have taken a different turn. The industrial free trade area might well have been established in 1958 or 1959, or Britain would have entered the European Economic Community in 1963.

It is at these points that the U.S. role was played. It is not difficult to understand why Americans should regard the establishment of a United States of Europe as the optimal formulation of European ideals. Quite apart from national prejudice, they, like the professional "Europeans," recognized the specific economic and political benefits of European integration.

In the early years after the war, the urgent needs were for a defence alliance across the Atlantic and for economic recovery in Europe. The contribution which the United States was required to make was primarily in the form of economic aid. Supply conditions in Europe were such that access to the North American market and the trade arrangements that such access might imply were bound to be of secondary importance. Professor Beloff's book[1] records some of the early discussions within executive and legislative branches of government in Washington. At first there was a concern only for cooperation, but in 1950 Beloff reports that the House of Representatives amended the Economic Cooperation Act to include among the objectives of American policy the encouragement of the "economic unification of Europe." Significantly, they at first included "and federation" in the above phrase, but the anticipation of progress via the Schuman Plan, which was conceived in 1950, caused U.S. legislators to delete the federalist concept on that occasion. However, the Atlantic Union Committee, founded by private citizens in the United States in the same year, began to press for consideration by the North Atlantic Treaty signatories of a North Atlantic federal union. Dean Acheson spoke at the time of closer association between Canada and the United States and the OEEC nations. George Kennan gave this a slightly different and more specific form. Describing Kennan's unpublished paper, Beloff notes[2]:

Apparently he suggested a form of organization under which a continental axis based on France and Germany, and more or less identical with what came to be the "Six" of little Europe, should co-exist with a United Kingdom-United States-Canadian axis which might also include countries on the Atlantic periphery of Europe such as Norway, Iceland, and Portugal. The main advantage of this alternative, as Kennan saw it at the time, was that the continental European grouping might still have had an attraction for the countries of central and east-central Europe, while it was out of the question that they would be permitted by the Russians to engage themselves in any organization which included the United States and Britain.

But, especially after the outbreak of war in Korea, Secretary of State Acheson was more concerned with anti-Communist alliances, and the Department had written off any longer-term prospect for cooperation with the countries of eastern Europe. In the early 1950s, the European Defence Community and the negotiations which culminated in the Rome Treaty focused attention on European integration, with America's commitment in the latter instance being limited to a blessing. The wisdom of a limited role was recommended by the EDC experience, when the United States committed itself extravagantly to support of the ill-fated proposal. American government officials were encouraged in their growing insistence that the

[1]Max Beloff, *The United States and the Unity of Europe*, Washington, Brookings Institution, 1963.
[2]*Ibid.*, p. 52.

European Economic Community represented the only appropriate vehicle of integration or cooperation. To be in favour of any other institution eventually almost constituted opposition to the EEC and thus to America's plan for Europe.

The most serious consequences of this attitude were those which affected Britain in the mid-fifties. As Beloff has noted, during the early stages of negotiations in the industrial free trade area idea proposed by Britain, the United States showed an open mind toward the proposal, provided that it was a means of forwarding unity in Europe. After the French counter-proposals of March, 1958, the U.S. State Department became concerned that the European grouping might be incompatible with GATT. But it was at the end of 1958, when the negotiations were on the brink of breakdown, that the Americans refused the request of several delegations to serve as mediator. There appears to have been division in the U.S. administration concerning the desirability of the free trade arrangement, with Dulles and Dillon being among those opposed. But it is at least doubtful that U.S. activity as a mediator would have carried the case after May, 1958, when de Gaulle came to power.

Part of the problem of U.S. policy-makers arose out of their preference for multilateralism and the avoidance of economic spheres of influence in the developing world. In an effort to make the EEC itself compatible with the preference for multilateralism, the United States eventually rationalized the position that only those regional economic groupings with political implications could be acceptable, and there was overt hostility to EFTA. As for the associate members among former French colonies, the United States was, to say the least, unenthusiastic about this form of discrimination. However, something approaching a double standard is reflected in their attitude toward Britain's membership in the EEC in 1962. Even though the Kennedy administration apparently had much better relations with the United Kingdom than its predecessor, Schlesinger reports that[3]:

When Macmillan revisited Washington in April 1962, the President made it clear that the United States was backing British membership for political not for economic reasons, that Britain must not expect to take care of everyone in its economic wake—either in the Commonwealth or in the European Free Trade Association—at America's expense. In particular, while we recognized the need for transitional arrangements, we could hardly accept a system which would give Commonwealth farm products a permanent position in the Common Market more favorable than that enjoyed by competing products from the United States.

In other words, the United States was prepared to permit to the associated territories of the EEC a special position in the European market which it

[3]Arthur Schlesinger, Jr., *A Thousand Days*, Boston, Houghton Mifflin, 1965.

was not prepared to see Britain's Commonwealth partners achieve, presumably because the Commonwealth countries supply more products which are competitive with those of the United States.

A further point which is implicit in the passage quoted is that the United States expected Britain to abandon its commitments to other countries, including the Commonwealth, in the interest of fitting into the version of European integration which the United States favoured. This would have been a more unreasonable attitude had not the United States demonstrated its desire to meet the challenge of the economically restored Europe by a positive trade offer of record-breaking proportions. The Trade Expansion Act of 1962, it should not be forgotten, could have led to an elimination of most important trade barriers between North America and Europe, and the U.S. failure to achieve its most ambitious aims is attributable primarily to a misreading of European intentions and not to any loss of determination on its own part. The United States was so convinced of the probability of British entry into the EEC that it based the dominant supplier authority of the Trade Expansion Act—which permitted elimination, and not just 50 percent reductions, of tariffs—on those categories of goods for which the United States and EEC accounted for 80 percent of trade among non-Communist countries.[4] Had the U.S. administration accepted the Congressional (Reuss-Douglas) Amendment, which would have included Britain and her EFTA partners in the calculation of the 80 percent categories, entry into the EEC would not have been essential to ensure substantial scope for negotiations under the dominant supplier authority. But the administration apparently considered that the narrower definition of its European trading partner would help to exert leverage on the British application, an implicit assessment of American influence on European integration which was clearly no longer warranted by 1962.

There gradually emerged out of the disappointment following de Gaulle's veto of Britain's application a recognition of the need for a new approach in transatlantic relations, or perhaps a new concept. This was paralleled by developments in defence arrangements. The complexities of defence planning are obviously too great for comprehension in a few sentences. It must suffice to note that certain changes in substance and attitude had occurred by the early 1960s. First, with the arrival of the ICBM, North America became as vulnerable as Europe. Second, the new regime in Washington had altered strategy in the face of the balance of terror and replaced the

---

[4]The general authority for tariff reduction was limited to 50 percent, and it was on this authority that the Kennedy round actually proceeded, because the U.S. and the *present* EEC members account for 80 percent of non-Communist trade in only two categories of commodities—aircraft and margarine.

massive retaliation approach with concepts of limited response and escalation. Third, the Cuban crisis of 1962 dramatized the probability of independent action on the part of the United States in the face of near and present danger.

These circumstances provided the reason, or perhaps the excuse, for the rise of the concept of a truly independent deterrent. The fact that this latter concept bore a French imprint reflected its peculiarly political motivation, and also the economic strength of France, which now made it possible to divert so many resources to that symbol of power. Although the French deterrent could have only limited effect and although the U.S. shield remained necessary to the balance of power in Europe, the independent French deterrent had certain clear potential apart from the symbolic, perhaps the most important being the trigger effect. It afforded the French a choice of occasion, though, to be sure, such an option could be exercised only once.

The United States soon recognized that its dominant role in NATO should be reviewed. The changing significance of the so-called independent British deterrent after the Skybolt "crisis" and the everpresent need to satisfy German sensitivities about their rank in the alliance further complicated the matter. The result was at first an experiment with symbols—the multilateral nuclear force (and the Atlantic nuclear force), which would stand for the equality of at least all the larger NATO nations. But no one was much deceived about the importance of such forces in the whole Western military position. The U.S. finger remained effectively on the trigger which mattered.

Subsequently there has been more attention to the real substance of an alliance of equals—the principles and machinery of consultation have been embodied in the McNamara Committee, and serious attention has been given both to contingency planning and to what Buchan describes as "a centre for the effective and continuous discussion of much broader questions, of forms of strategy that are most likely to keep the peace, of proposals for arms control that will avert future crises, or of the political objectives which the western powers should pursue." The Berlin crisis of 1961–62 is cited both as an illustration of the careful working out of alternative responses to the range of possible circumstances and as an occasion on which there was a lack of consensus among allies on broad political objectives. Buchan is forced to conclude that "NATO has no system of collective decision-making that would stand the test of a major world or European crisis."[5] He and others have been led further to propose

[5]Alistair Buchan, *Crisis Management*, Boulogne-sur-Seine, France, The Atlantic Institute, 1966, p. 44.

that the reality of American power and the complexity of the U.S. government probably mean that any increased role for NATO allies in those many, and often only indirectly related, decisions which affect them will require the presence in Washington of various diplomatic and military groups of representatives of NATO countries. Buchan further stresses that "only continuous relations with American officials who are part of the American planning process will satisfy European governments and lead to effective conclusions."[6]

Thus, if it is to survive and adapt to the new circumstances, NATO as a military alliance has to become even more "transatlantic" in nature. The fact that the present and foreseeable future challenges to both North America and Europe may arise in far distant parts of the globe would appear to accentuate the importance of close and continuing consultation among NATO members.

As already noted, the political and economic development of the early 1960s gave rise to a shift in terminology. The concept of Atlantic partnership arose and, in Washington's hierarchy of images, replaced Atlantic community. It seemed to correspond better with the realities of the post-postwar period and permitted independent European positions while asserting the necessity of joint endeavours. It also conveniently reduced the need for U.S. commitments to economic and political integration. The United States could never hope to attain a special pre-eminence in such a group such as she was likely to continue to hold in the military alliance and its decisions.

Is "partnership" in economic and political matters compatible with "community" in the military sphere? The answer to this should be in terms neither of abstractions nor traditional institutional relations, though it must account for both. Some Europeans will argue that a European defence community is still possible, though probably only if Germany is an equal partner. But it is doubtful that any of the main powers involved would be prepared to see such an independent group built in western Europe unless the problem of German unification were first settled. And conditions of unification for an armed Germany which would be acceptable both to the United States and the USSR would surely be rather difficult to conceive. German unification is more likely to occur if Germany remains a nuclear-free *protégé* of at least one of the superpowers, and then most likely in circumstances of *détente* between the United States and the USSR.

If the Atlantic military alliance, so long as it continues, is likely to remain a community rather than a partnership, what implications has this for economic and political matters? Surely here one must identify content.

[6]*Ibid.*, p. 46.

What do we really mean by Atlantic economic community? Lower tariffs or no tariffs? OECD-type cooperation, or a free trade area, or a customs union, or an economic union, or a federal union?

On the European side, interest in Atlantic community has fluctuated. In general, the smaller countries have an open mind toward any degree of transatlantic integration. They have no national aspirations which could be better served by rejecting interdependence. If their preoccupations are with Europe, it is because their present opportunities rest in that integration of Europe which is already under way, and many of their intellectuals are still excited by the hope of political integration. The Benelux countries and Italy want most of all to preserve the EEC and, if at all possible, to realize still more fully the aims of the Rome Treaty. In general, they would not oppose any extension of EEC membership or participation of the EEC in a larger Atlantic arrangement, unless such a move were to destroy what they have already built. For Denmark, its primary concern for agriculture products and its divided trading interests make some form of rapprochement between EFTA and EEC highly desirable. For the rest of EFTA, larger (and, in the case of the neutrals, looser) groupings are generally preferred to smaller. It is only the three largest west European countries whose positions are more complicated and, except for France, their attitudes toward "Atlantica" correspond quite closely to those of the smaller nations. They value both Atlantic military alliance and European economic integration. They are clearly interested in cooperation through OECD and could be expected to meet proposals for freer or free trade with an open mind, but they would likely resist the development of supranational institutions. Ironically, both de Gaulle and some of the "Europeans"—those with the most federalist inclinations—are most disturbed by possible incompatibility of Europa and Atlantica. As already noted, their reasons differ, but ultimately they both fear that Europe cannot realize its highest aspirations if it is sublimated in Atlantica.

One of the most troublesome aspects of the European attitude to transatlantic economic relations is the feeling about U.S. investment. The European view, let it be said again and again, is more than 90 percent mythology. Part of the problem is the alarm with which old politicians and unsuccessful European competitors regard the success of American products on European markets. They fail to recognize this as an indication of the degree to which Europeans now want and can afford to have North American goods. One disturbing aspect of the situation is that some European industry has taken the view that U.S. competitive ability is dependent upon the size of corporations. As those European businesses which have become established in North America have discovered, there are highly successful corporations in most industries which are very modest in size. If they pursue "giantism" as the magic formula, they may suffer disillusionment and a fit of despondent protectionism. Surely the great advantage of U.S. firms lies in their ability to exploit a large market, to develop large-scale production of specialized products, for which the development and fixed production costs can be spread over substantial output. The large corporation is often the result—the sometimes embarrassing result—of success, and *not* the essential cause of it.

Fortunately, most European governments have not adopted a restrictionist attitude toward U.S. investment, and only in France has it been carried very far. The fact that the government of France has been so concerned about U.S. investment is undoubtedly related to its view about the U.S. balance of payments relationship with Europe. The view that the United States must reduce its capital outflow and thus resolve its alleged balance of payments deficit before any real setttlement of the international monetary situation is a politically convenient one, though almost void of economic meaning. In the first place, it implies that the United States should raise interest rates, a policy that has to a degree been adopted. However, the interest gap has generally been maintained by the parallel actions of European central banks. Secondly, any substantial deflationary action by the U.S. government would imply an economic policy position and consequences which no democratic government, and certainly not those of Europe, would risk. Thirdly, the alternative of U.S. devaluation or European revaluation is rejected by both European and U.S. governments. U.S. authorities (public and private) now question the existence of a U.S. deficit deserving further interference with the flows of goods and capital. However, if one takes account of the flows being restrained by current U.S. policy, a case for revaluation or devaluation, recognizing the effects of European recovery, may still be argued. The United States prefers to stress the inadequacy of European capital markets. One solution to this problem, to which both European and U.S. governments could have made more effective contribution in the last ten years, would have been the effective integration of the U.K. economy in Europe and the consequent freeing of London's financial institutions from the sterling confidence problem. However, the heart of the problem lies in a lack of agreement on the international adjustment mechanism and in an unwillingness to increase the independent role of the IMF, a matter which will be discussed shortly. It suffices here to conclude that monetary cooperation does not now provide a hopeful base for transatlantic economic integration.

The United States, to its credit, has never resisted European integration. Quite the contrary, it has most approved those forms of integration with the deepest implications. This has been because of the U.S. belief in the importance for world peace of west European integration. There have been reservations about the economic implications—both the competitive strength of European producers once they adapted to the supplying of the vast market and the danger that the European market might not be made accessible to U.S. exporters. Once the EEC was firmly established, the United States left no doubt of its willingness to engage in far-reaching trade negotiations with the Community.

However, certain aspects of the U.S. position raise doubts. The first of these is the tendency to centre U.S.-European policy so much on the EEC. The reason has clearly been the preoccupation with "the German problem." But even if the support for the Community and related institutions has been fully justified, does this mean that the United States should have rejected other expressions of European unity or approaches to economic integration? The end product of failure to push the industrial free trade area and of pushing too hard for British entry into the EEC appears to have been to weaken the U.S. bargaining position today. U.S. policy-makers may be afraid to alter or diversify their strategy now, lest it is taken as opposition to the EEC or merely a petulant reaction to de Gaulle's eagle-plucking.

But other aspects of U.S. policy also have a bearing on this. One is the preference for multilateralism dating from Cordell Hull. This is firmly based on the desire to avoid discrimination and the conditional and bilateral arrangements which so disturbed interwar trade relations. The continued U.S. allegiance to a GATT-only technique in trade policy fitted well with the scope of U.S. power and responsibility in the world. However, GATT itself recognizes the validity of varied approaches to the same objective, with the customs union and free trade area techniques having been quite widely adopted or considered for adoption. The U.S. attitude toward participation in such a grouping has been governed by fear of its consequences for relations with non-members—for example, the fear that the United States would cut itself off from Japan or be blamed by the developing countries for creating a rich man's club if it joined even the most comprehensive Atlantic grouping. This attitude neglects the use of the free-trade-area approach as a strategy for attaining broader objectives.[7] As will be stressed later, far-reaching cooperative action by the industrially advanced countries may be required if any substantial response to the demands of the developing countries for trade concessions is to be possible.

[7]In any case, participation in a free trade area (as opposed to a customs union) does not need to restrain a country from exchanging concessions with non-members, and may well encourage it, particularly if they are used as stepping stones toward extension of membership.

Others claim that the real reason for U.S. reluctance to contemplate free trade areas is an unwillingness to make such a far-reaching commitment to free trade. When the protectionist lobbies are active, such a commitment may seem impractical. But it must be remembered that Congress gave the President authority under the Trade Expansion Act of 1962 to eliminate tariffs on a wide range of products, including many categories of chemicals, machinery, motor vehicles, etc. It may be argued that no one anticipated that the United States and the EEC and its main trading partners would actually eliminate these tariffs. Nevertheless, if the commitment could be made once, it could be made again, provided the political arguments for a new initiative were again of comparable importance. It is difficult to argue that the economic cost to U.S. industry (or to the U.S. economy generally) would be a substantial deterrent to liberal trade, especially now that the U.S. government is committed to adjustment assistance.

The key questions about the future course of international economic policy are two: (1) Will there be sufficient motive to warrant any new trade initiative on the part of the United States? (2) If that motive exists, how will the United States and its trading partners respond—by the reassertion of established postwar policies or by some new venture or approach? The answers to these questions may be to a degree implicit in the foregoing, but what is lacking is an appraisal of the role of the Atlantic nations in the world. There are still reasons for promoting cooperation and even integration among the advanced nations of North America and Europe for the sake of peaceful economic relations within this region, but the most compelling considerations of the next few years may come from problems and needs which are not primarily, or at any rate not exclusively, of North Atlantic origin.

4. A World Economic Role for Atlantica?

Before assessing the economic role of the Atlantic countries, it is well to stress the constraints imposed by the relative mobility of resources. Some resources or economic inputs—natural resources and fixed capital—cannot be moved. Populations are more mobile, but it is difficult to imagine a world in which all barriers to migration are removed, especially between the wealthy and poorer regions. Furthermore, many people will not move, even if all legal and economic barriers are eliminated. Technology and money capital move quite freely, except for man-made restraints. Apart from the equalization of economic opportunity achieved through the movement of these latter resources, the efficient allocation and use of the world's resources depends upon the movement of goods. Thus the international economic policies of the advanced nations bordering the Atlantic are likely to focus primarily upon two areas: policies to promote economically sound capital movements and monetary stability on as broad a basis as possible, and trade policies which can be more regionalized but which must exploit, or at least take account of, any opportunities for multilateral trade liberalization.

Integration of the world economy has taken many historic forms. The colonialism of the nineteenth century permitted integration between advanced European states and groups of dependent economies. Between these, goods, money capital, and even people moved freely, but particular developmental decisions were in the hands of the governments and enterprises of the colonial powers, and the dependent peoples lacked opportunities for equivalent access to skills (technical and entrepreneurial) and thus often to capital. In the twentieth century, nationalism and rival imperial regimes meant that the flow of capital and goods between advanced countries was restricted. Only after fighting two wars have the European states returned to the search for an economic *modus vivendi*, this time by regional economic groupings, encouraged not only by bitter lessons of the past rivalry, but also by the challenge of a new imperialism from the East. At the same time the coming of nationhood in the colonies has changed the character of trade and other relationships between them and the North

Atlantic countries. They have rejected imports of manufactures, insisted upon capital, technical, and entrepreneurial "know-how" on their own terms, and now want preferential market access for their own manufactured exports and guaranteed stability for their income from primary production.

In 1967 the world may be visualized as having four industrially advanced focal areas or nations, bordered by two groups of fringe countries—those that are advanced but not integrated, and those that are less developed. The "focal area" countries or groups are (1) the USSR, (2) the European Economic Community, (3) the United States, and (4) Japan. Each of the above groups, except Japan, contains in the neighbourhood of two hundred million people. Advanced "fringe" countries are more or less closely associated with each of the above: some of the east European satellites (Poland, Czechoslovakia, and perhaps Hungary); the EFTA countries; Canada; Australia and New Zealand. Except for the EFTA group, these countries are all relatively small compared to the focal-point countries. If Britain's economic position were stronger, EFTA might well be comparable to Japan's group, though its smaller and less homogeneous and less compact nature means that its role is subordinate in Europe. The prospect of Austria and perhaps Denmark breaking away to join the European Economic Community reflects all these considerations. It is its instability which particularly distinguishes EFTA from the so-called "focal areas." Of course, there are other distinctive features of these fringe countries or groups which should be mentioned—the ambiguous nature of economic integration between the east European satellites and the USSR, Britain's association with the overseas Commonwealth, the isolation of Australia and New Zealand.

The less developed countries are also to some extent grouped around the focal points, though even less distinctly than the advanced fringe areas. Some, like the AOTs of the EEC and the less developed Communist countries of southeast Europe, such as Bulgaria, have a clear connection with the focal areas, while others like the Latin American countries are tied to their focal area (the United States) more by economic aid and political affiliation than by special trade arrangements. The position of the developing Commonwealth is affected by the uncertainty of the future role of all the advanced Commonwealth countries and by the large size of some of the Asian members. The Western Hemisphere members are small enough to be fitted into any trade arrangement based on North America (or with Canada alone). The African Commonwealth could follow Nigeria's lead into association with the European Economic Community. But the large Asian members, India and Pakistan, like China and Indonesia, are not readily related to any focal area. Their problem of economic development and their social and political evolution and influence are likely to be a continuing concern of all the focal areas and a reason why the political relationships between them may remain unstable as long as the battle against poverty in that region continues.

The reason for the foregoing formulation of world economic groupings is to place the Atlantic countries in the broader economic context and thus to identify the dimensions and scope for Atlantic action in international economic matters. As indicated in the earlier chapters, many of the problems of Europe and North America can be resolved by efforts at unity within those regions. But on some issues, interaction is inevitable. One of these already discussed is relations with the Communist countries of eastern Europe. Cooperation between the United States and the EEC in dealings with eastern Europe could produce a very different consequence from a competitive approach, particularly in the context of differing views of American strategy in other parts of the world, notably the Far East.

Similarly economic relations with Japan present a continuing problem, though clearly Japanese political preferences and their involvement in such predominantly Atlantic institutions as OECD and GATT seem to insure a stable relationship with Japan for the present. Any closer Japanese association with either or both of the Atlantic focal areas would probably depend as much on Japan's willingness to adapt its unique business organization and public policies to the requirements of Atlantic economic integration as on the willingness of the Atlantic countries to cooperate.

The far-reaching questions which would appear almost insoluble without Atlantic cooperation are two: international monetary stabilization and a non-discriminatory trade strategy for dealings with the developing countries.

The reform of the monetary system

The efforts of recent years to strengthen and supplement the International Monetary Fund have arisen out of two principal concerns: dissatisfaction with the method of providing international reserves and a lack of consensus on the role of exchange adjustment in the international adjustment mechanism. A third aspect, which takes on a character of its own, is confidence in the reserve currencies, though, at least so far as the dollar is concerned, it is unlikely that this problem would be distinguishable from the other two in origin or independent of the particular implications for the dollar of any sterling crisis. Most of the discussion of these issues to date has centred on the role of the reserve currencies. As hinted earlier, the interpretation of the U.S. balance of payments situation by European central bankers and by some political leaders has clouded the issue. Part of the problem is purely political—the unwillingness to continue to accept the U.S. dollar as the principal international reserve currency. Part is the result of a dubious view that the U.S. deficit is a phenomenon requiring deflationary corrective attention. When account is taken of the statistical peculiarities of the U.S. deficit, of the special effect of U.S. international political commitments, and of the unique role of U.S. capital markets as long as completely inadequate alternative sources of capital are available in Europe, it is more difficult to make a case which would warrant demanding U.S. deflationary action as, in effect, a firm condition for further international cooperation on the improvement of the world monetary system.

Those Europeans supporting such a view seem to be saying that the United States should engage in deflationary action of the sort which the Europeans would themselves find it politically difficult to justify under similar circumstances, and that only after the United States has taken such action will they be willing to cooperate further in supranational reforms such as those proposed by Triffin and others. Yet if the growth of reserves were limited by U.S. action to alter its balance of payments position, a serious strain might be placed on reserves before facilities to meet the need were established. The extension of IMF reserves and the stand-by credit arrangements developed to avoid sterling crises undoubtedly help considerably, but if U.S. gold reserves were to be further depleted, whether on economically justifiable grounds or not, such arrangements could break down. Many people consider that the United States has the ultimate weapon, that it could stop dealing in gold without fear of a breakdown in international exchange, because most people would be perfectly prepared to hold U.S. dollars. This view is by no means universally held in Europe, though it is always difficult for those who demur to identify what anyone could do, in retaliation to a U.S. gold embargo, for actions of this sort would injure the position of other countries as much as, if not more than, that of the United States. It is, in any case, the U.S. sense of responsibility for world monetary stability and reluctance to exacerbate relations with continental Europe in any way, as well as a well-known Congressional nostalgia for "solid gold" money, which will ensure the continuation of efforts to temporize and to accept the "Group of Ten" stalemate.

Perhaps even more fundamental is the lack of consensus on the adjustment mechanism. The two principal means for long-term international monetary adjustment are relative inflation (or deflation) and the exchange rate. However, control of capital movements and other exchange controls, while intended as temporary devices during postwar reconstruction and balance of payments difficulties, have become a common substitute for these more fundamental adjustment methods. The International Monetary Fund permits exchange rate adjustments of up to 10 percent without formal approval, and of larger proportions with such approval. In fact, following the first few postwar years, this form of adjustment has seldom been used. After postwar recovery, the relative strength of Europe's economy vis-à-vis North America was much improved, and revaluation seemed appropriate. However, it is always a difficult move to adopt, and the changes made in European currency values have been minor. Whether relative inflation has been adequate to account for the remainder of the adjustment is a matter for argument, since it is clear that neither the Europeans nor the United States have found it easy to impose on domestic political priorities the requirements of international adjustment by this means. Many economists argue that if all the interventions initiated by the U.S. government to alter the balance of payments were abandoned, it might become clear that U.S. "devaluation" is required and that this is a much better approach to the adjustment problem than the manipulation of capital movements and of aggregative economic policy purely to satisfy the requirements of international equilibrium. Since it is not at all clear that Europe would acquiesce in a U.S. "devaluation," the approach is often labeled impracticable, but as already hinted, it may be a question of choosing a time and method.[1]

One must conclude both that Atlantic agreement is essential to any long-term remedy of the shortcomings of the international monetary mechanism and that there is little prospect of a reconciliation of views in the near future. Cooperation in this sphere may have to await some success from collaboration in other policy areas between North America and Europe.

Economic policies for the developing world

In the past, relations between the industrially advanced countries and the developing world have centred on capital aid and technical assistance. Multilateral and bilateral efforts have progressed hand in hand, though often without anything approaching an ideal pattern of priorities. Disillusionment has not been uncommon as Sisyphus' rock of economic growth has been slowly and unsteadily pushed up the hill made steep by population increase and bumbling efforts at national (and nationalistic) economic planning.

There can be no doubt that large-scale economic aid has still a top priority. The foreign exchange gap and the short-term consequences of growth policies make it essential that external aid flows should continue and indeed should grow. But the practical political problem in donor

[1]See Robert Mundell, *The International Monetary System: Conflict and Reform*, Montreal, Canadian Trade Committee, 1965.

countries requires that everything be done to ensure that aid efforts are efficient and are seen to be efficient. With this in mind, the new stress on trade policies by the developing countries is of double importance. The U.N. Conference on Trade and Development in 1964 highlighted several aspects of the trade question, of which three are most significant: (1) the call for free access for tropical products in the markets of the advanced temperate countries, and for the avoidance in the latter of discriminatory taxation on such commodities; (2) the call for measures for stabilizing income from primary products, such as commodity agreements and compensatory finance schemes; (3) the call for tariff preferences on imports of the manufactured products of developing countries entering the markets of the advanced countries. These are all put forward as means for ensuring, through trade policy, the efficient use of resources in the developing countries and the avoidance of uncertainties and hardship arising out of fluctuations in production of primary products.

The Atlantic world has had little difficulty in responding to the first of the demands. Substantially free access has been granted to tropical products and domestic taxation on them has been cut.

The other two requests are less easily met. Stabilization schemes have in the past encountered many difficulties. International commodity agreements must be carefully designed if they are to avoid the problem of uneconomic pricing and vast surpluses.[2] However, in general the Atlantic countries have shown a willingness to look once again at the various alternatives for ensuring stabilization of income in the primary industries. There are indications that the long-term trends in this type of income may not be as unfavourable as the representatives of the developing countries have sometimes claimed. Recent market conditions have clearly improved, though this cannot be taken as a reason for assuming that stabilization efforts are no longer required.

The main issue which was raised by the UNCTAD conference was the proposal for preferences for manufactured products. This was based on the argument that, to encourage appropriate specialization in manufactures in developing countries, they should have preferential access to the markets of the industrially advanced countries. Otherwise, it is claimed, they could not for some time compete against the manufactures of other advanced countries. It is a version of the "infant-industry" argument for protection. There has been much discussion[3] of the potential importance of such

[2]See W. E. Haviland, *International Commodity Agreements*, Montreal, Canadian Trade Committee, 1963.
[3]Harry G. Johnson, *Economic Policies towards Less Developed Countries*, Washington, Brookings Institution, 1967.

preferences. Some have claimed that the barriers to imports in the developed countries are not so great as to bar imports, given the great labour cost advantage of the developing countries. Against this, it has been pointed out that the practice of graduating tariff rates, with the higher rates on the more completely manufactured products, discriminates very markedly aganst imports of such products. A tariff of 10 percent on import value represents a much higher rate of protection on the portion of value added in manufacturing in the protected industry. (If the value added is one-third of the value of the product, the effective rate of protection becomes 30 percent.) In any case, it is the long-term or "dynamic" implication of the removal of such barriers which would probably be most important to the development pattern of the less developed countries (LDCs).

At the same time, economic spokesmen for these countries have been criticized for giving less attention to the specific form of the preferences. First of all, if these are determined primarily by the present patterns of tariffs between industrially advanced countries, it is by no means clear that preferences based on these hodge-podge schedules would encourage the sort of manufactured exports for the LDCs which would make the best use of their resources. Secondly, if the developing countries themselves retain very high levels of protection, manufacturing industries with export prospects will have to compete for inputs with those whose existence is justified only as suppliers of limited and protected domestic markets.

A practical trade strategy which will meet the needs, if not the demands, of the developing countries will be difficult to work out. The industrially advanced countries will be reluctant to retain the tariffs which restrict trade between themselves, primarily for the purpose of affording preferences to the LDCs. This is particularly true for those countries which are not yet part of a free trade group, since a real commitment to preferences would bar them from joining or forming such a group. Furthermore, the concept of preferences runs counter both to the principle and past practice of the GATT. The GATT countries have already agreed to pass to the developing countries, without full reciprocity, the concessions which they decided to exchange after the Kennedy round negotiations. It seems unlikely that these will satisfy the LDCs. Since the AOTs of the EEC already enjoy preferential access to the EEC markets, the United States could set up a parallel arrangement with Latin America to provide preferences for this group of countries. But in view of U.S. interests in the Pacific and elsewhere, this would not appear sufficient. Furthermore, there would be domestic political resistance in the United States to a policy of providing unilateral free access which was not also adopted by other advanced countries. Clearly there is a much greater probability of offering free access to developing country manufactures if the United States can act jointly in this respect with other countries. This would be even more so for other advanced countries not already part of a larger free trade grouping (Britain and Canada, for example), since their manufacturers would feel more exposed to the impact of new imports than would those of the United States. Of course, it will be argued that Britain already gives substantially free access to Commonwealth manufactures, including those from Asia. The fact that the elasticity of supply in the developing countries is likely to be low for some time will not allay all fears. It seems probable that a broadly based effort to meet the demands of the developing countries would be welcomed by the latter even if it did not include explicit preferences except against those advanced countries which failed to participate. For that matter, some preferences could be attained by devaluation of developing-country currencies when appropriate, though the developing countries themselves have resisted this means of establishing preferences.

Any agreement among some or all North Atlantic countries, and perhaps Japan, to grant free access to manufactures from developing countries might be accompanied by some form of condition or incentive encouraging the developing countries to form free trade areas among themselves and after an appropriate period to reduce their tariffs more generally. By this means they would be encouraged not to waste resources in the duplication of industries among themselves and in the misuse of resources for high-cost production activities supplying only domestic markets.

Toward a realistic policy program

The foregoing comments suggest how difficut it is to devise a program for trade and development which accommodates even the essential economic and political interests of the countries involved. Any proposal made in this area is bound to be criticized. If it is a modest and piecemeal "inching forward" from the present practice, it will be condemned as inadequate and unbalanced. If it is bold and far-reaching it will be regarded as unrealistic.

The principal requirements of any effective program on the part of the industrially advanced countries include at least three:

(a) It should be substantial enough to contribute to economic development, assuming that relevant domestic policies are adopted by the developing countries themselves. This probably means that the program should be sufficient to make at least a perceptible difference in the growth of income per capita and, ideally that it should improve the prospects for closing the gap between living standards.

(b) The program should have some prospect of acceptance by the developing countries. It should encompass the kind of opportunities for the governments and industries of those countries which can be exploited without requiring unrealistically large changes in the political "sophistication" and social preferences of the people. This relates to the kind of strings attached to the aid programs and the adjustments required to realize the benefits of trade policies. Domestic reforms which affect the social base of the power structure will be resisted, and governments will cling to some form of "infant-industry" protection against import competition from industrially more advanced countries. More generally, in the early stages of independence, the desire to reserve a wide area of discretion in the choice of economic policies (comprehensive or at least ubiquitous economic planning) is likely to tax the ingenuity of aid donors and of GATT members seeking to introduce relevant economic criteria into the development process. The least objectionable means of achieving this aim would appear to be through introducing as much as possible of the impersonal force of international competitive specialization, at least among the developing countries themselves, and where such impersonal forces must be replaced by external managerial decision, as in aid and loan policies, the international agency would appear to be more acceptable than the national bureaucrat or private investor as the source of advice and interpreter of investment integrity.

(c) Finally, the program must take account of the differences in attitude among advanced countries and must seek a basis for the largest measure of agreement, while avoiding frustration through seeking or expecting unanimous support for a particular program. At the present time there is clearly a limited base for joint action by the European and North American countries. GATT and OECD are the principal arenas for formulation of common initiatives covering trade, aid, and development. OECD is a useful forum especially for the consideration of criteria and scope of foreign aid, but it continues to depend on implementation by national governments. GATT has already made the kind of contribution which its principle of non-discrimination permits. Its likely role in the near future is as the conscience of its members, reminding them that discriminatory policies adopted for the purpose of economic development place in jeopardy not only GATT itself but also the long-run efficiency of the pattern of development. The fundamental issue is how to make the most useful contribution to development through trade policies while preserving the long-term multilateral objective.

Without pretending to have a unique solution for so comprehensive a problem, one can perhaps illustrate the kind of compromise with reality which could conceivably find general acceptance:

1. The further development of the EEC-AOT relationship, one "trade-and-development" region already established. Two immediate issues which this region faces are the role of Britain (and EFTA) and of the Commonwealth countries of Africa. The implications and probabilities relating to British entry have already been explored. The prospect of African members of the Commonwealth becoming Associated Overseas Territories of the EEC clearly depends only partly upon British membership. The negotiation between the Nigerian government and the EEC won a modified form of association for the largest African Commonwealth member, and Britain played very little role in those negotiations. Most members of the African Commonwealth would be welcomed by the EEC, but some would undoubtedly be somewhat less interested if Britain is unsuccessful in its new bid. Of course, their attitude would depend on the extent to which they can retain access to both British and continental markets. The Asian Commonwealth is most unlikely to obtain similar access to the European market, because it is a much more important supplier of manufactured goods.

2. The development of a Western Hemisphere "trade-and-development" region. The formation of a free trade grouping comprehending the present Central American Customs Union and the Latin American Free Trade Area, and including even those countries not now members of these groups, is being discussed. The participation of the United States in discussion on this subject will undoubtedly focus on the possibility of a measure of unilateral free access to the U.S. market for exports from Latin America, including exports of manufactures. Meanwhile there is considerable interest among the Caribbean members of the Commonwealth in a free trade arrangement with Canada, and some response evident in Ottawa. Whether Canada could join the United States in offering unilateral trade concessions to the rest of the Western Hemisphere is unpredictable. It would clearly depend upon the nature of the arrangement and the implications for Canada's other trade relationships. It is relevant to note that the whole of Latin America and the Caribbean has a population of over 200 million, which means that it approaches the combined population of Canada and the United States. The EEC with 175 million people is larger than the African Associated Territories, which have less than 100 million, or about 150 million including Nigeria. If EEC and EFTA were combined and all former British territories except South Africa were to become associated, the ratio would be about 275 million in Europe to about 210 million in Africa. This has very little significance as an indication of the capacity of the developed regions to absorb the impact of development. GNP would be

a better measure. Here the ratio of combined Canadian and U.S. productive power to that of the EEC-EFTA combination was, in 1963, about $600 billion to $350 billion. Although the Latin American productive potential is undoubtedly greater than that of Africa for the near future, it is not so much more as to make it harder for the countries of North America to assist the development process through trade and aid policies. In any case, the higher wealth per capita in Latin America should make it possible for this region to generate a higher percentage of its own savings, and the tendency to develop trade among Latin American countries, though still infirm, could make a major contribution to efficient development.

If British efforts to enter the EEC are unsuccessful, the development of special north-south commitments will not take place in the same way. Britain would undoubtedly attempt to maintain existing Commonwealth preferences as long as other Commonwealth members wanted them. Her capacity to do this and the interest of those who benefit from preferential access to the British market would depend on the strength of that market. If under these circumstances a larger free trade association were established by the United States, Canada, Britain, and those EFTA countries who remained outside the EEC, the north-south relationships could be more complex. All the members of the association might be willing to agree to give parallel trade concessions to the African Commonwealth and Latin America. In all probability this would mean that fewer former British colonies in Africa would seek associate status in the European Economic Community.

An interesting aspect of the African situation is that there has been less tendency to form free trade groupings, though several have been suggested and one or two have survived the break-up of jointly administered groupings, the most notable being that between Kenya, Tanzania, and Uganda. Insofar as trade groupings should economically, and can politically, cross linguistic boundaries imposed by the colonial past, competing attractions would exist for some former British colonies. Although there is little apparent movement toward free trade groupings among West African countries, such groups might more readily develop if all these countries were overseas Associates of the EEC. However, if Britain is not a member of the EEC but becomes a part of a larger and more open-ended association, it is likely that Commonwealth Africa would regard the benefits of access to the North American as well as the British market as more attractive than any intra-African arrangements. To conclude these speculations concerning Africa, one should admit that the greatest probability lies in the continuing drift of African states into "EEC Associate" status, whether or not Britain enters the EEC. Any other alternative would depend on a commitment on the part of the United States to unilateral reduction of trade barriers comparable to that embodied in the Rome Treaty. Such commitments do not appear to have received serious consideration in Washington even for Latin America.

The British Commonwealth relationship extends also to Asia, where it presents a more difficult problem. India, Pakistan, and Hong Kong are already important producers of manufactured goods. European countries, apart from Britain, have been most reluctant to permit imports of these goods. There is bound to be considerable pressure for some kind of arrangement to meet the needs of these countries for export outlets, and the loss of access to the British market which would accompany British entry to the European Community would greatly heighten such demands. But the requirements of Asian development do not indicate regional solution.

3. A vital role for GATT is implied by two aspects of the above. On the one hand, the demand for a new trade institution may well grow if GATT does not satisfy the needs of the developing countries. On the other hand, there is no apparent reason for a new institution provided GATT contracting parties make full use of the scope of the agreement to meet the changed requirements of the present time and accommodate the new methods employed. GATT combines resolute support for the principle of non-discrimination with a recognition of the fact that non-discrimination is not an end in itself, but rather an important guarantee that the benefits of trade liberalization will be disseminated as widely as possible. Article 24 is the best indication of the latter. Unfortunately, some supporters of GATT have lent support to the view that regionalism is necessarily opposed to multilateralism. Such a view fails to take account of the diversity in size, degree of economic development, and historic dependence upon trade among the nations, and also the patterns of cultural and political affiliation. There may be an opportunity for GATT to sponsor a program of unilateral concessions on the part of the industrially developed countries which would take account of regional north-south arrangements. If, for example, western Europe continues to develop its association with most ex-colonial territories in Africa, and the United States and Canada were to move in the same direction with Latin America, GATT negotiations might focus on agreements between Western Hemisphere and Euro-African groups working towards two objectives:

(a) The reciprocal reduction of remaining barriers between developed members of the two groups, and perhaps between developing countries; and the exchange of unilateral concessions to developing members, the EEC reducing barriers to Latin American exports in exchange for U.S. and

Canadian reduction in barriers to African exports. It should be reiterated that, while these north-south arrangements will not involve reciprocity in dismantling of trade barriers, the developing countries might be expected to accept certain terms: limits to the level of their trade barriers, and possibly a program of devaluation combined with reduction of import restrictions. As already hinted, the willingness of developing countries to form free trade areas among themselves could well be an appropriate accompaniment of unilateral concessions by the advanced countries to the north.

(b) The working out of a program of concessions to non-Communist Asian countries—India, Pakistan, Indonesia, etc. The great difficulty in achieving this objective lies in the necessity of joint action, preferably among all developed countries. The EEC has shown little interest in providing Asian countries access to its markets. It might be possible for the United States, Canada, Britain (if not a member of EEC), and Japan to act without the EEC in this regard, and possibly the USSR and some eastern European countries might be induced to make parallel concessions in a different form. In the face of the challenge from China, all these countries may come to share a more common, if competing, interest in contributing to economic growth and political stability in southeast Asia.

To succeed with this sort of approach, the GATT signatories and secretariat will have to shift their emphasis considerably. Perhaps a new associate status will have to be established to extend the direct participation of developing countries. Clearly, much more study will be required of the impacts of *potential* exports by such countries on the markets of the developed countries under circumstances in which all of the latter are making concessions. Realistic appraisal of supply elasticities would help to reduce fears arising out of the uncertainty associated with such changes, and the consequent tendency to exaggerate the capacity of countries such as India to produce in large quantity the kind of goods demanded in the United States or Canada. Clearly, the ability of leading GATT countries to achieve any of these objectives will depend on joint action. Two new forms of joint action can be suggested in implementing the aims just discussed: the working out of agreements between European countries and the advanced non-Communist nations, designed to expand trade opportunities, especially in manufactures, between them; and most fundamentally, the development of a common approach among the advanced market-economy countries. The idea of an industrial free trade area encompassing all of these who wish to join seems the technique most compatible with GATT and likely to provide the market scope and consequent competitive efficiency which would enable the members more readily to absorb the impact of imports from developing countries.

While the foregoing discussion certainly suggests the complexity of the challenge facing GATT and its signatories, it should also have brought out the remarkable fact that GATT as it now stands is fully equipped institutionally and by precedent to foster the arrangements heretofore outlined. It has accepted free trade areas and customs unions as an exception to the principle of non-discrimination. It has emphasized in principle and in practice that regionalism means must serve the ends of multilateralism. It has recognized that a distinction may be drawn in trade negotiations between developed and less developed countries and that reciprocity is not essential in dealings between countries at different stages of economic development. While the ingenuity and flexibility of GATT signatories and of the secretariat will be severely tested if these principles and precedents are to provide the foundation for a successful trade strategy in the coming years, the neglect of the challenge to create a "trade and development" strategy may well mean the atrophy of GATT and its replacement by new institutions or by a period of stagnation in trade negotiation activity.

4. Complementary financial requirements and the role of OECD. Although the main purpose of this study is to identify the role of trade policy, it must be recognized explicitly that financial flows (through external aid and international investment) and balance of payments arrangements play an essential and complementary role. So long as one is dealing with economic relationships among industrially advanced countries, it is relatively easy to separate trade matters from development policies and programs. Investment decisions are typically decentralized; and in the absence of serious balance of payments difficulties, the supply of savings flows comparatively easily across international boundaries. The main focus in OECD activity has been on the U.S. and British balance of payments. Underlying much of the contention in the IMF and OECD working parties, there has been the role of the U.S. dollar as a reserve currency and the desire of some Europeans to reduce reliance upon U.S. capital. But neither this nor the discussions of liquidity arrangements nor the appropriateness of the adjustment mechanism has much affected the flow of goods or capital across the Atlantic. Basic confidence in the dollar remains unshaken. The relationship between capital flows, trade, and exchange rates is much more explicit where developing countries are involved, since capital movements are so much more directly determined by government, and the exchange rate or reserve position is less likely to be regarded as primarily economically determined. Thus in preparing a common position on development aid and related policies, OECD countries can ill afford to neglect the role of trade policy. Aid and investment programs may make a much more limited contribution if formulated and applied in isolation from trade

measures, and both trade and aid policies can be frustrated by domestic and exchange rate policies which hamper efficient specialization. It must therefore be hoped that the OECD could work in close collaboration with GATT and with those of its members endeavouring to sponsor regional north-south arrangements, with a view to identifying those balance of payments situations requiring support through aid and exchange adjustment for the purpose of realizing the intermediate- and long-term developmental benefits of industrial specialization and trade.

In sum, there is a very great challenge facing the advanced countries. There is little doubt that an appropriate trade strategy could do much to contribute to more economic patterns of development in the world's poorer nations. But there is also little doubt that a substantial response to the developing countries' demands can be made only if the economically more advanced nations act in concord. Herein lies one of the most compelling reasons for joint future trade policy action by the countries of the North Atlantic area. Nor would it appear to be a challenge which can long be avoided with impunity.

5. Canada's Choice:
A Summary of Prospects and Options

Canada cannot often expect to exercise a determining influence upon the choice of international economic policies, though it has a very much greater potential influence upon such policies than nations many times its size in population. This is so because Canada is fifth among the world's trading nations and because it is the chief partner of the country which, more than any other, determines economic policy in the non-Communist world. Canada's government must be aware of the meaning of any major commercial policy change for the nation's economic growth and for the welfare of its people, as well as for the role the country wishes to play in world politics.

Since the end of the war there has never been a time of greater uncertainty in world economic policy. It would be easy to be pessimistic about the future. But a time of uncertainty is a time of choice. And when the great nations are in some confusion and are recalculating their course, there is an unusual opportunity to affect the choice. Professor Harry Johnson said recently that "Canada alone holds the key to the resolution of the present deadlock in international commercial diplomacy."[1] Whether or not one values Canada's possible role so highly, there can be no doubt that it is vital now to understand our options and to discover our opportunities. What is likely to happen?

A conservative prospect

In order to reduce to a minimum the number of alternatives which one need consider, a limited or "conservative" prospect will be sketched out. Reasons why departure from this choice may become necessary will then be examined. Finally, the question of Canada's interest in supporting the conservative option or departures from it will be explored. This procedure seems warranted because it is increasingly clear that a conservative forecast is likely to be a realistic one. There is a weariness with initiatives in the

[1]In a speech delivered to the Canadian Club in Montreal in October 1966; he was supporting the statement issued by the Canadian American Committee in June 1966.

world's capitals and even in its international organizations; all seem pre-occupied with defending positions against traditional enemies, even though many realize that the nature of the problems has changed. Of course, there are always good reasons for conservatism. In the current setting, these include the mortality of de Gaulle and Mao and the fact that with the passage of time the militancy of Soviet Communism seems increasingly to be tempered by economic prosperity.

Forecasting is a risky business, but if one must choose a "most probable" course for international economic policies over the next few years, it might be as follows: a slower tempo for efforts toward economic integration and cooperation, especially among the North Atlantic countries, and a series of efforts, some perhaps successful, to respond to the demands of the developing countries.

WEST EUROPEAN UNIFICATION: A SLOW MARCH

In particular, within the Atlantic region, as implied in the earlier discussion, the evolution of the EEC even after de Gaulle will probably be more gradual and will be lacking in the sense of economic opportunity and political necessity which brought the Community into existence and carried it through the early years. Gradual progress in the coordination of agricultural, transport, taxation, and other policies within the Community should be possible, though there is little evidence that the absence of coordination (except in agriculture) is regarded by the members of the Community as a serious handicap to the realization of the benefits of the customs union. This "lowering of the sights" of integration may make it easier for the EEC to accept new members, or associate members, particularly Austria and Denmark, and conceivably Spain and Portugal. However, three factors will continue to make British entry difficult—the problem of adapting British agriculture and food prices to the terms and implications of the common agricultural policy, a concern on the part of the Commission and of other continental governments about the British distaste for supranational institutions,[2] and the French reluctance to share leadership on the continent.

There is little doubt that at present certain features of Britain's relationship with the United States might have to be modified to satisfy the Gaullist conception of the appropriate role of western Europe in world affairs.

[2]If the parliamentary base for EEC activities could be strengthened, some British opinion would be won over, and while the Commission would be more than content to see this happen, much continental and British opinion would not welcome the depletion of national legislative sovereignty.

EAST-WEST RELATIONS: A THIRD FORCE?

Further western European integration also depends upon the events governing East-West relations within Europe and upon the course of political and military relations between the United States and Europe. A conservative expectation is that while closer trade relations between East and West are likely as a consequence of the liberalization of foreign trade practices in eastern Europe, political change will be slow. Neither West Germany nor Britain has shown any propensity to exchange its place behind the American shield for a western European defence grouping. Any Soviet offer of German reunification is unlikely to be made in terms which would encourage Germany to throw aside the NATO shield or to permit it to rust away. But there are at least two factors which may bring about a greater East-West *rapprochement* within Europe: first, the concept of a European third force, which is continuously advocated not only by de Gaulle but also by those with more truly "European" outlook, and secondly, the present unenviable U.S. position in Viet Nam, which encourages a falling away of the support of allies even where the latter have no convincing alternative solution to the dilemma involved.

As and if the United States and China come to occupy the ends of the world political spectrum, it may be increasingly in the interest of the Soviet Union to encourage the third-force idea, and even to offer German reunification on terms which would be difficult to resist—conceivably even a western European defence grouping in which Germany as a whole might participate, but with a much looser association with the North American members of NATO and perhaps with a non-aggression pact with the Warsaw Pact countries. Britain would have less to gain than Germany from such developments, but it might be difficult for British political leaders to resist the pressures to which they would be exposed under the circumstances. In the present state of the Viet Nam conflict, no matter how one assesses the merits of U.S. policy, the possible implications for Europe cannot be ignored.

THE UNITED STATES AND EUROPE: SEPARATE ROOMS

The role of the United States, not only in European and Atlantic affairs but on the whole world stage, continues to be of fundamental importance. The arenas in which U.S.-European relations are currently being determined are NATO, GATT, the Group of Ten, and OECD. Of these, the first two are most important. The efforts of the Group of Ten and IMF to achieve a better consensus on monetary matters constitute a holding action; as for durable adjustment, national authorities remain unwilling or unable to achieve a common diagnosis of the world's monetary ills and (or) unwilling to place more confidence in the IMF.

OECD is an auxiliary institution whose future depends upon the success of the more explicit efforts toward economic integration. NATO and the GATT are the loci of real commitment. NATO is in disarray because of its success, and one of the consequences of success may be the relative decline of the institution which gave rise to it. One may argue, as it often is argued in Washington, that the dangers in Europe have dwindled in size and changed in form but have not disappeared. This view will for some time have sufficient validity that the Treaty will remain in force. But as already noted, the change in the nature of the balance of terror and of European attitudes toward it makes it most unlikely that NATO will be the basis for closer political or economic integration of the North Atlantic countries, and it is even doubtful whether the present degree of defence integration can be maintained.

The Kennedy round of GATT negotiations has been the most active arena of transatlantic economic relations, and noteworthy progress in the dismantling of trade barriers affecting industrial materials and manufactures has been achieved. The negotiators were able to claim that cuts on industrial tariffs averaged about one-third, with 50 percent cuts in quite a number of categories. Many U.S. and EEC tariff levels were reduced to between 5 and 10 percent, promising new market opportunities for exporters willing and able to absorb taxes at these levels. Clearly de Gaulle and other European leaders felt that their interest in an independent political position would not be compromised by acceptance of industrial tariff cuts. They did not take the same view of the agricultural negotiations, which ended with the anomalous claim that some measure of success was reflected in the promise of a higher price for wheat! The economics of agricultural trade negotiations staggers the imagination.[3] The other basis for disappointment in the Kennedy round lies in its failure to achieve the original aims of the Trade Expansion Act. But since this was inevitable once Britain had been denied membership in the Community, Washington had become reconciled to the measure of success in terms of a substantial fraction of the 50 percent reductions permitted under the most general provisions of the Act. With the electorate and public leaders primarily concerned with other issues, the scaling down of expectations can be accomplished with comparatively little political hardship.

[3]The issues in agricultural trade policies will be discussed in David L. MacFarlane and Lewis W. Fischer, *The Prospects for Trade Liberalization in Agriculture*, to be published later in this series.

There are now good reasons for expecting that commercial policy will be put on the shelf in Washington for some time after the Kennedy round— according to some observers, at least until after the presidential election of 1968. It is difficult to imagine that Congress will be much interested in extending a significant new authority to the President, especially since he did not use the full authority available to him under the 1962 law. Indeed, at the end of 1967, the problem is to prevent backsliding through quotas and other non-tariff barriers designed to evade the Kennedy round concessions. Nor will President Johnson be likely to ask for new legislation. Both Congress and President are concerned with domestic racial tensions and intractable problems of conflict in Asia, and America's chosen partner in Europe has proven indifferent to the world's larger issues, as the United States defines them, and fractious on those which directly concern transatlantic relations. The best way to avoid making a bad situation worse may well appear to be "separate rooms." More specifically, Atlantic-minded Americans and Europeans will be tempted to wait until de Gaulle has left the stage.

In trade policy particularly, the most ardent supporters of the traditional GATT approach are also likely to favour a period of waiting or, at most, of probing for deals in particular commodity sectors. There are some indications that the GATT secretariat itself will encourage a go-slow approach, because any substantial progress might have to be by regional free trade arrangements, and some of the most zealous supporters of GATT have always been apprehensive about massive resort to Article 24.

THE DEVELOPING COUNTRIES: THE PREFERENCES QUESTION

What will this tendency for pause in trade policy mean for the developing countries? They can at least enjoy unilaterally the concessions granted in the Kennedy round. They have already obtained free access for almost all tropical products, and success in commodity agreements and other techniques for price and income stabilization on behalf of primary producers may not depend on progress in tariff reductions. But, as suggested previously, this is not likely to satisfy them. Ever since the first UNCTAD conference, the trade-policy spokesmen for the developing countries have emphasized that access to markets for the manufactured goods they want to produce is as essential as development aid. They were among the first to express dissatisfaction with the outcome of the Kennedy round and argue that the market access they require cannot be assured without preferences. Can the industrially advanced countries respond positively to these demands?

For the United States the challenge is particularly difficult, since preferences of the kind requested run counter to the U.S. desire for multilateral solutions. The Associated Overseas Territories of the European Community already enjoy preferences relative to non-members of the Community. It would be almost impossible for the United States to grant parallel preferences to other developing countries, though Latin America might seem to be a candidate for such special treatment. At the Puenta del Este meetings in the spring of 1967, at which the principle of establishing a Latin American common market was approved, the United States indicated a willingness to grant temporary preferences to be removed by the subsequent elimination of tariffs on goods from developed countries. U.S. interests and commitments in Asia and even in Africa are such that a position favouring imports from Latin America, which to be meaningful would have to include a continuing obligation to retain other trade barriers, would be objectionable from the viewpoint of countries whose economic and political future are of great importance to the United States. And if the United States were to contemplate granting relatively free access to her markets to the manufactures of all developing countries, perhaps excepting the AOTs, such a scheme would encounter resistance in the United States unless other advanced nations were willing to cooperate in some such scheme. The other key countries outside the EEC, including Britain and Canada, would not be likely to expose their economies to manufactures from a wide range of developing countries on a basis which required the preservation of trade barriers between themselves and the United States. In any case, these countries, and Britain in particular, already offer substantially free access to a considerable range of manufactured imports from such important developing countries as India and Pakistan. Thus the scheme that seems to appeal to some Europeans, under which spheres of trading interest would be established—the EEC in Africa, the United States in Latin America, and perhaps Britain in Asia—is unrealistic from the viewpoint of non-EEC nations for economic as well as political reasons.

An alternative acceptable to both the United States and the LDCs is difficult to identify. An arrangement by which the non-EEC advanced countries (and later the EEC) jointly and unilaterally would grant free or freer access to their markets for manufactured exports from all developing countries, while exchanging similar concessions between themselves, might be feasible. But this would not create a preference position and might be regarded as inadequate by developing countries. There is, however, one way by which preferences might be achieved in this context: by the devaluation of some or all of the currencies of the developing countries at the same time as the above-mentioned trade arrangements were being effected. Since devaluation is not likely to receive enthusiastic reception in the developing countries, and probably not in the IMF, the prospects for U.S. support for any long-term preference scheme are limited.

One may question whether the United States need go that far to meet the demands of the developing countries. A general move to liberalization among many (or all) industrially advanced countries, accompanied by unilateral concessions of the same order to the LDCs, would be difficult for the latter to reject as insufficient, especially if accompanied by an appropriate international aid and investment program. Indeed, the bargain might appropriately include some incentive to developing countries to establish regional groups among themselves so as to avoid the worst excesses of diversification of manufacturing activity in nations with very limited domestic markets.

The great importance of the developing countries in the foreign-policy planning of the United States will make trade and aid policies a matter of continuing consideration in the future. The whole range of policy discussions—aid programs, commodity stabilization arrangements, and efforts to dismantle trade barriers affecting development—will continue. Perhaps the cotton textile agreement may be used as a prototype for other schemes to control the growth of manufactured exports from the LDCs and to calm the fears of "high-wage" industry concerning the scope of these imports. But it is difficult to be sanguine about the prospects for a bold U.S. initiative. There is little indication that the United States is likely to make trade commitments to the developing countries, especially those outside the Western Hemisphere, comparable to the commitments made by the European Economic Community to its Associated Territories. It seems quite probable therefore that other developing countries will follow the lead of Nigeria and seek to negotiate associate status in the EEC. Under certain political circumstances described earlier, this drift in the trade affiliation of developing countries could further reduce the influence of the United States in Asia and Africa and would also reduce the remaining significance of economic aspects of the Commonwealth.

Are other options available?

The availability of an international commercial policy alternative would appear to depend primarily on the U.S. attitude to a commitment in the trade field comparable to those the United States made in the 1940s respecting military and monetary matters. In military matters, because of the overwhelming importance of the American deterrent, the United States has not hesitated to commit itself to international alliances which, though not universal in membership, have provided a basis for bargaining from strength with the Communist countries and a foundation for peacekeeping activities in all parts of the world. In monetary matters, the United States willingly undertook an international commitment, and the importance of the dollar in the first fifteen postwar years made it unnecessary to question the adequacy of the IMF. With the advent of the U.S. balance of payments problem, however, some aspects of this commitment have proved more embarrassing, though to its credit the United States has never wavered in its support. It has chosen to bide its time, getting agreement on methods of putting out fires but postponing the erection of a fireproof building. If anything, in the interest of preserving the *status quo* in the monetary club, it may have gone further than was economically warranted in attempting to "correct" a balance of payments problem which many non-governmental economists consider of doubtful importance.

In trade policy, no comparable commitment has existed. GATT is a basis for negotiation, not a comprehensive commitment to reduce trade barriers, though it was made explicit at the outset that at least certain types of barriers ought to be removed. Congress has given the President a varying power to negotiate but never a long-term commitment to substantially free trade. The original content of the dominant supplier authority of the Trade Expansion Act implied that the United States would be prepared to go to zero for certain categories of products if the EEC reciprocated, and the United States apparently believed that this provision would be effective. But this arrangement left the President free to determine how far the United States should go as the negotiating positions of its trading partners were revealed.

The traditional arguments against a more explicit U.S. commitment to free trade have been, first, the difficulty of getting domestic political support for it; second, the lack of economic importance of any such move to the United States; and third, the belief that U.S. international aims could as well be attained by other means. The Trade Expansion Act of 1962 demonstrated that if international motives were strong enough and political leadership effective and determined, the weight of the first argument is reduced. As for the second argument, the direct role of foreign trade in the U.S. economy is unlikely to exceed 6 or 7 percent and has usually been closer to 5. However, the access to the markets of Europe, Canada, and Japan and ability to meet the competitive challenge are now of much greater importance to the health and strength of U.S. goods-producing industries than in the past. And above all, the economic burden the United States has accepted in the developing countries can be reduced by trade policies which encourage more effective use of external aid and investment in those countries, and by a sharing of the implications of those trade policies with other advanced nations.

Finally, the alternative means of achieving U.S. aims in the world have diminished in relevance and effectiveness. In relations among the advanced countries, the dominant importance of the defence alliance in NATO has been diminished by its success and is clearly not the basis for extending the area of economic and political cooperation or integration. The increasingly recognized need to find a common North Atlantic basis for developing relations with eastern Europe provides one important motive for a common trade commitment by the Western market-economy countries. The stalemate in international monetary matters may be difficult to overcome so long as the balance of payments positions of the United Kingdom and the United States are misinterpreted in Europe and treated with palliatives and postponement. A trade commitment involving the United Kingdom might not be sufficient to remove the need for a better understanding and consensus regarding the appropriate adjustment mechanism, but by strengthening the British economy (including its capacity to serve as a European capital market) and the bargaining position of both the United Kingdom and the United States, it might at least bring the discussion regarding monetary arrangements back to the relevant economic options. Finally, as already stressed, a trade commitment by which the United States and its main trading partners granted access to their markets to the manufacturers of the developing countries not only would go far to meeting the needs of those countries, but also would more than match the opportunities open to the AOTs of the EEC because it would be non-discriminatory.

Probably the most obvious form for such a trade commitment would be a free trade area open to all developed countries and adopting as one of its central features a unilateral offer to the developing countries,[4] modified only by some incentive to economic cooperation or integration among the smaller developing countries themselves. The initial offer might also incorporate agreed guidelines for expanding and "liberalizing" trade arrangements with non-market economies.

The two big problems associated with such a proposal would be the policy for agriculture and the role of the EEC. These issues are closely interrelated. Unless the free trade area concentrated initially on industrial goods, the prospect for eventual EEC participation would be severely reduced. A common agricultural trade policy of the free trade area countries should also be worked out on a liberal basis but, if possible, with an

---

[4]This proposal was supported in the Canadian-American Commitee statement, *A New Trade Strategy for Canada and the United States*, June 1966.

institutional framework which would enable the aligning of EEC agricultural policy with that of other industrially advanced countries, once the EEC countries have made progress in rationalizing their own agriculture.

The last few paragraphs are offered as an indication of the sort of U.S. commitment which might meet the new realities in world economic relationships as well as accommodate established institutions.[5] Before turning to Canada's interest in supporting or rejecting such a proposal, one must assess the relative prospects of the conservative outlook discussed earlier against those of any new initiative. As already hinted, the conservative option has for some time now seemed much the more likely. The reasons lie largely in Washington: the preoccupation with Viet Nam, the fear of adopting any approach which might be interpreted as antipathetic in the European Economic Community, and the reluctance to make a trade commitment comparable to the NATO and IMF commitments of the past. As already indicated, good arguments can be developed for a "standpat" position. A few years could alter some circumstances in directions which will favour the old policies. But, as also indicated, some circumstances have probably changed in directions which demand new policies or substantial modification of the old—reduced momentum of European integration, the British problem, the prospects for economic relations with eastern Europe, the nature of the developing countries' "demands." If the United States relies on its past framework for meeting these challenges, there is a very real possibility that its prestige and its influence in all these regions may be reduced in the years ahead.

There are many, even in Canada, who will accept such a prospect with equanimity. But even for them it poses a question about Canada's option, given the degree of interdependence which actually and inevitably exists between Canada and the United States.

Canada's international interests

Unlike the United States, Canada is interested in international economic relations because of their importance to the Canadian economy and standard of living and not primarily because of their contribution to international peace and stability. However, the latter is important to Canada too, and though Canadian attitudes in world politics have usually been closely identified with those of the United States, Canada has a number of unique political interests.

[5] A third option, which will be discussed later, would be a purely Canada-U.S. free trade area. It is assumed that this would have much less relevance for the larger international issues discussed in this section.

The most traditional of these is the Commonwealth association. Much has been written about the decline in the importance of the Commonwealth. The political and economic ties which bound all members to Britain are clearly weaker now, and the nationalism of the developing countries has highlighted their individual rather than their common interests. Yet it is precisely because of the implications of self-determination and economic development that old and new members are clinging to the Commonwealth concept and trying to fashion it to the needs of these times. It is almost trite to note that Canada, as the principal ex-colony in the "old" or "white" Commonwealth, has a unique opportunity to find the means of ensuring close collaboration between the "developing" and "developed" worlds. Issues such as Rhodesia pose challenges but also provide opportunities with wider implications. On the economic side, Canada can set an example through its per capita contribution to external aid. Fortunately the political atmosphere in Canada is now favourable to such a policy, notwithstanding the short-term political and economic constraints of national budgeting.

But since the UNCTAD conference of 1964, the developing countries have indicated clearly that the benefits of aid are severely discounted if trading opportunities are denied them for those product lines of which they are, or can become, competitive producers. The problem facing Canada and Britain particularly is how, within the Commonwealth, to meet these demands for preferential markets when their own needs may require the reduction of trade barriers vis-à-vis other industrially advanced countries. It would appear necessary to act in conjunction with the United States or other developed countries. As already noted, the EEC is the only large group of such countries which at present offers such preferential access to the developing countries, but it also seems unlikely that the EEC can or will afford similar access to Asian or Latin American countries. The advantageous position of the present AOTs and of those other countries which are permitted to join the group is most likely to keep this issue alive unless some response is forthcoming. Commonwealth conferences may provide a forum in which proposals can be worked out, but they cannot be realized by the Commonwealth alone, given the dimensions of the development problem. One may conclude that Canada's relationship with the Commonwealth remains important because it is a constant reminder that the world's greatest political and economic challenges are no longer North American or North Atlantic in origin; but the very dimensions of the problems, especially in their economic aspects, mean that the Commonwealth must be primarily a forum or a "workshop" in which ideas requiring wider applications are hammered out.

Canada also has an interest in continental Europe which differs in origin and character from that of the United States. First, there are the cultural associations with France, which have taken on a new meaning in the province of Quebec in recent years. Second, there is the greater relative importance of European markets, especially for Canadian exports of industrial materials and foodstuffs. These considerations mean that Canadian governments will tend to elect policies that maintain and develop transatlantic associations. At the present time, however, there is little which separates Canadian and U.S. interests. Both wish to maintain the NATO alliance; both are concerned about the possibility of inward-looking European trade and economic policies. Neither government has shown much capacity to devise new approaches which would encourage the more outward-looking attitudes of some of the EEC countries, or at least of some European leaders. In the United States there appears to be a fear of any approach which might conceivably be interpreted as antagonistic to the EEC or which might be disruptive of the delicate situation in NATO. In Canada, the sensitivity about French feelings on the part of Canadian political leaders has sometimes seemed exaggerated, as in the hesitancy over relocation of the political headquarters of NATO. Canadian government leaders must, of course, take into account the sympathy which exists among substantial numbers of Canadians (and not only in Quebec) for French views on China and Viet Nam, though one might hope that Canadian energy might be diverted to more constructive Canadian initiatives in these areas.

In any case, differences between Canadian and U.S. attitudes toward continental Europe would appear to have little bearing on economic policy alternatives, and the many parallel interests seem to point to opportunities for parallel or joint action.

Canadian relations with the Communist countries have more distinctive elements. Canadians have never been convinced of the strategic value of restraints upon trade in the vast majority of products which embody little or no defence technology. Canadians feel that their exports of wheat to eastern Europe and China are justified not merely on the "fast-buck" argument sometimes advanced in the United States, but also on the basis of that East-West trade which happily now is seen, even in the United States, as a basis for long-term coexistence and *rapprochement* of economic systems. The further development of these trade relations will encounter many difficult obstacles. For Canada, the large trade surplus will mean continuing pressure to develop imports and all the consequent difficulties of dealing with centrally planned economies. The development of East-West trade will be assisted by the tendency of eastern European countries to decentralize control of foreign trade and even of the related production activities, but the problems associated with dumping and stability of contracts will remain. It is likely to be in Canada's particular interest that techniques for approximating economic criteria in these trade relations be worked out, whether by the western Europeans or by the Atlantic or GATT countries more generally.

In sum, Canada's international role incorporates a wide variety of political and economic interests. Many of these she holds in common with other countries, but in some respects the Canadian role and Canada's opportunities are unique. First, Canada's close economic relationship with the United States is far more than a cliché. Not only is the United States by far Canada's chief trading partner, but Canada is also by far the principal trading partner of the United States. The differences in the proportions are great, but there are times when it is the relative role that counts most, and this includes all those occasions when trade policy can make a vital contribution to the solution of international problems. Every time that the United States faces the necessity of a new decision in trade policy, Canada has an opportunity. Furthermore, a similar case may be made for the importance of capital movements between Canada and the United States; and insofar as our experience with foreign capital provides guides for the role of international capital flows more generally, Canada can offer useful advice. Canadians are, however, under some obligation to teach lessons based on fact rather than on prejudice and on unwarranted generalization from particular instances.

Second, an independent Canadian political voice in world affairs is vital. Those varied economic and political interests just described are only one reason for such a role. More important is the belief within Canada that national identity is best embodied in a voice from the North American continent which is not French nor British nor American in accent, but which, in a paraphrase of Mackenzie King, may be "not necessarily different, but different if necessary" from all. Canadians may nowadays be doubtful about the importance of their role in world affairs and even a little cynical about the capacity of Canadian governments to fill it, but one thing is clear: other countries, particularly in the developing Commonwealth, still look to Canada for understanding and assistance in making their case at the United Nations and in Washington and on occasion will accept from Canada an interpretation of Washington's or London's views which they would be less likely to acknowledge from the source itself.

In proceeding to discuss Canada's choice among trade policy strategies we should therefore bear in mind, first, that in trade questions the Canadian voice can be important and, second, that Canada's commercial policy choices should not be made without reference to the role Canada can play as a leader of the middle and smaller powers. This implies that among alternative trade strategies, those which encourage trends toward multilateral trade liberalization are preferable to Canada, other things being equal.

Canada's options

Among the alternatives which have been identified in earlier discussion, three may be singled out for evaluation on the basis of the above criteria: (1) a continuation of efforts to reduce barriers exclusively through GATT's traditional bargaining processes, with full application of the most-favoured-nation provisions; (2) an approach to multilateral reduction via the free-trade-area approach, encompassing all those countries prepared to participate; (3) an application of the free-trade-area approach on a strictly regional basis, encompassing Canada, the United States, and perhaps other countries of the Western Hemisphere.

None of these alternatives necessarily contravene the General Agreement on Tariffs and Trade, though the question whether they would encompass substantially all trade would determine whether there would be objections by non-member countries. For example, under all three the special treatment of trade in agricultural products might reduce the commodity coverage, but objection could hardly be taken to this, given the precedents established by EFTA and the EEC.

Canada's choice among the three would depend in part upon the foregoing political preferences and in part upon the implications of each for Canada's economy. The latter have been evaluated in a number of studies dealing with the impact of free trade on particular industries or regions.[6] Evidence available to date supports a view widely held by Canadian public authorities, by many spokesmen of private industries, and by those professional economists who have paid particular attention to the problems of Canadian industry. This view is that, at the present stage in Canadian development, schemes which provide for the virtual elimination of trade barriers would be much more advantageous than further limited reduction of such barriers, provided that this would be fully reciprocated by the United States and preferably also by Canada's other principal trading partners, and provided also that a period of transition is assured and that appropriate transitional policies are instituted to assist the adaptation of Canadian industries to the new challenges and opportunities. Furthermore,

[6]The analyses of the implications for particular industries and regions incorporated in the studies of the Atlantic Economic Studies Program will be available during 1968. See also Ronald and Paul Wonnacott, *Free Trade between the United States and Canada: The Potential Economic Effects*, Cambridge, Mass., Harvard University Press, 1967.

even for those industrialists who are still reluctant to see Canadian trade restrictions dismantled, the partial reduction of barriers (sometimes referred to as the "strip-tease" method) by the traditional GATT method is regarded as more damaging to their interests than a free trade area with appropriate transitional safeguards would be.

This conclusion is based on the argument that the Canadian market has now grown large enough that efficient specialized production facilities for a wide variety of manufactured goods can be located in Canada primarily on the basis of the market available in Canada. Further, it is noted that the reason why many manufacturers are still unable to compete with imports without protection is not the consequence of any fundamental disability but rather the result of the effect of protection itself—both foreign tariffs and other forms of protection which prevent Canadian producers from achieving efficient production on the basis of an export market and Canadian trade barriers which support an inefficient structure of supply in Canada. This latter characteristically takes the form of several producers endeavouring to supply small amounts of similar and competing products exclusively for the Canadian market, with no one, therefore, able to achieve the scale and specialization of production which access to the whole Canadian market or to export markets would make possible. This set of circumstances is set forth not as a general theory of Canadian manufacturing practice, but rather as an indication that the current inability of some Canadian firms or industries to meet international competition on even terms is no indication of what might be possible if Canadian industry were adapted to exploit the opportunities which fuller access to North American or world markets and competition with foreign producers would afford. Furthermore, it illustrates why commercial policy changes might have to be substantial to be of any use at all.[7]

The generality of the circumstances just described remains to be demonstrated. However, in defending the Canada-U.S. automotive agreement, the government itself has indicated that it believes the structural problems of this particular industry can be solved by a scheme for aiming at the elimination of trade barriers, though the nature of the transitional arrangements and uncertainty about the extent of the commitment that will prevail after 1968 have raised some doubts about the economic merits of the scheme. The government has also hinted that other programs having the same basic rationale and purpose might be initiated for other industries. Representatives of many of these industries have from time to time indicated

---

[7]The argument contained in this paragraph is more fully developed and supported in my *Industrial Structure in Canada's International Competitive Position*, Montreal, Canadian Trade Committee, 1964.

approval of free trade, at least with the United States. Hence the increased interest not only in the areas traditionally supporting free trade schemes— the western provinces and the Maritimes or Atlantic provinces—but also in central Canada, the heartland of Canadian manufacturing. Clearly opinion has changed in Canada. Analysis is still very much needed to determine to what extent the new view of commercial policy requirements is warranted, in which industries the opportunities are as described, and in which industries the costs of adjustment might be so great as to raise questions about the political or economic desirability of facing the challenge posed by free or freer trade. Above all, there is the most difficult question: are the general costs of adaptation such that it would be many years before the benefits could be enjoyed? These are issues whose answer depends on the whole range of studies being undertaken in the Atlantic Economic Studies Program and on other complementary studies.

OPTION 1: THE FURTHER APPLICATION OF MFN

For this present assessment of commercial policy prospects, it must suffice to ask, if Canada elects a substantial change in its trade policy, which of the available alternatives is likely to suit best her needs? The further exploitation of the GATT negotiation techniques employed in the past would in many respects appear the most appropriate. Since the inception of GATT, Canada has been a principal advocate of the most-favoured-nation generalization of concessions. But as noted earlier, like NATO, GATT has by its very success altered its opportunities. The piecemeal reduction of tariffs was well suited to the early rounds of GATT negotiations, when tariffs were, in any case, much higher than needed to provide effective protection to the industries of the signatory countries. In 1962 a new method was suggested—"linear" cuts and attempts to achieve reciprocal elimination of barriers affecting certain categories of goods. By this means it was hoped that the real adjustment problems that might be raised by further substantial tariff cuts in some sectors would be balanced by opportunities in others and that political resistance to the acceptance of adjustment would be broken down by the generality of the cuts and by the adoption of adjustment assistance policies and the staging of tariff reductions. However, the Canadian government made it clear from the outset that it could not participate on the same terms in this type of negotiation. If a general cut of 50 percent (or any substantial percentage) in tariffs were to be agreed upon, Canada would face much more serious adjustment problems than would the United States or the EEC. The government argued that, for Canada, linear cuts would expose many Canadian firms now equipped to supply only protected domestic market to an import challenge they could not meet, while the linear reduction of foreign tariffs, even by as much as the 50 percent originally hoped for, would not be sufficient to warrant restructuring of Canadian industry toward a greater reliance upon the supplying of specialized exports. Only in those cases where the post-Kennedy round foreign tariffs would be low enough so that Canadian exporters might absorb them without placing themselves at a great competitive disadvantage would such restructuring be likely to prove economic. The Canadian government therefore offered a much more heterogeneous package of proposed tariff concessions which, it claimed, was equivalent to the linear cuts contemplated under the principle embodied in the U.S. Trade Expansion Act—"equivalent" in the sense that it would make a comparable contribution to the expansion of trade. This kind of argument will obviously apply with greater force to further partial tariff reductions through GATT negotiations.

Part of the problem with the GATT approach has always been that it was vulnerable to reversal or to the suspension of concessions. While in the 1962 Act an effort was made to reduce the possibility of this by allowing for gradual reduction of barriers and by adjustment-assistance provisions which would reduce the likelihood of circumstances leading to escape action, GATT concessions still remain susceptible to changes in the congressional or parliamentary winds in Washington and elsewhere and to retaliatory reimposition of obstacles to trade. It is particularly important for Canadian industry to find a means of securing trade concessions in a form which will assure it of long-term access to foreign markets and thus reduce the uncertainty which would otherwise threaten investment and production plans based on export opportunities. This is a consideration which favours treaty arrangements, since, on the past record, these are less susceptible to reversal through legislative action than are concessions granted by administrations on the basis of specific legislative authority. These comments have, of course, been applied particularly to the legislative process in Washington. A treaty encompassing the objective of elimination of trade barriers probably also affords a better context for the harmonization of those administrative customs practices which have frequently been used to frustrate the realization of the benefits of tariff reductions.

The recent statements by GATT spokesmen that further trade negotiations may take on a sectoral form raise particular problems for Canada. There is some logic to an effort to eliminate both tariff and non-tariff barriers on a range of related products, but such an approach also presents real difficulties, especially for a country such as Canada. In the first place, any one sector, such as chemicals or machinery, may be far more important in a particular country's exports than in its imports and force adjustments which would not be required if sectors having opposite balance of payments implications were also included. Secondly, unless all raw materials and intermediate goods are covered in the sector approach, the reduction of tariffs on a final-products sector may result in negative effective tariffs for the sector in question. Some evidence of this problem has been reported in the wake of the Canada-U.S. automotive trade agreement, where certain inputs remain protected even though those classified as auto parts have been freed of trade barriers. A final feature of the sector approach is that it is likely to leave protected a hard core of industries which would resist sector deals but which could more easily be covered in linear tariff cuts or broad free trade groupings.

But even assuming the possibility of one or two sector deals, especially in industrial raw materials, the prospect for further substantial GATT negotiations after the Kennedy round seems rather limited. Until the EEC's common market is more completely established, the member countries are not likely to regard further dismantling of their external tariffs as a high priority. If, then, Canada wishes anything more than a standpat policy on tariffs, or at the very best a deal covering one or two commodity sectors, the traditional GATT approach may well prove of limited significance for Canada. This does not, of course, mean that there need be any abandonment of the principle of multilateral trade liberalization or of the most-favoured-nation application of such concessions. It merely means that Canada must turn elsewhere if it seeks a route to more substantial reductions of tariffs and other trade barriers, particularly those affecting manufactures in which Canada has the largest unrealized productive potential.

OPTION 2: A GENERAL INDUSTRIAL FREE TRADE ASSOCIATION
The free-trade-area approach,[8] applied in its broadest and most open form, is one technique by which the multilateral aims of GATT can be fostered. The greatest advantage of the free-trade-area approach is that it does not depend for substantial success upon virtual unanimity among all signatory powers of the GATT. Its great danger is that it can result in competing or conflicting trade blocs if any important trade group is motivated to, and can afford to, practise exclusivity. The free-trade-area approach is likely to be most favourable in its effects if those who adopt it can thereby swing the balance of forces toward liberalism through the bargaining power they accumulate in establishing the bloc. Alternatively, a free trade area can

[8]Free trade area is used here instead of customs union or more advanced forms of integration because it is the arrangement which permits retention of the greatest degree of national autonomy in economic matters and thus would be likely to have wider application than the customs union, common market, or economic union.

benefit a particular region without adversely affecting the pattern of world trade if it enables the member countries to move more quickly toward a pattern of specialized production which accords with that of a freer trading world and thus increases their propensity to participate actively in multi-lateral agreements or in broader free trade groups. These two uses of the free-trade-area approach can be illustrated by the two examples already mentioned.

If the United States and Canada were to propose a general free trade area of developed countries, with appropriate unilateral concessions to the developing countries, this could help to swing the balance of world opinion in favour of general trade liberalization. It would constitute an invitation which the EFTA countries, Japan, and the EEC could not for long ignore. Those countries and established regional groups which favoured such a trade policy trend would be strengthened, and those which were hesitant would be encouraged to reappraise their attitudes. In Canada, the wide variety of Canada's political and economic interests in the world would be likely to assure much support for the proposal. In Britain, as already noted, the opportunity to integrate British industry more effectively in the world economy and thus perhaps to supply the essential ingredient which has to date been absent in efforts by successive governments to restore confidence in the pound is likely to be a compelling argument for seeking a new policy alternative to membership in the EEC, when and if Britain decides it can wait no longer for membership in the Community. There is, of course, the additional argument that the availability of an alternative would improve the likelihood of Britain's acceptance by the Community.

Clearly, everything depends upon the possibility of a bold initiative by the United States to make a commitment to elimination of explicit trade barriers by clearly defined stages. If there were a clear Canadian interest in an initiative in this direction and an indication of British and other EFTA support (which would have to be a private indication, given the present circumstances), the United States could, with Canada, launch the proposal, confident that even if no countries other than the two in North America, the United Kingdom, and two or three other EFTA nations participated, the grouping would have a great impact on tilting world trade policy toward liberalism of a sort that would be relevant to those problems which commercial policy may be helpful in solving—the economic and political uncertainties of Britain and outer Europe and the market requirements for sound growth in the developing world.

However, it must be admitted that the outlook for a U.S. initiative, or for U.S. response to a Canadian initiative, along these lines is not promising. As suggested earlier, the United States is preoccupied with Viet Nam, a pre-occupation which may be understandable, though a great power is unhappily never in the position where failure to act or to act wisely in one direction is likely to be excused by a more immediate priority. The United States more than most countries is aware of the needs and demands of the developing countries but has found it difficult to struggle to maintain its aid program and has apparently as yet found no broad basis for responding to developing country demands for trading opportunities. The key to rigidity or stagnation in U.S. policy appears to lie in the policy for Europe and the Atlantic.

At the heart of U.S. policy in recent years is the view that it is necessary for the United States to wait for European unity before proceeding with any attempt to develop an Atlantic community. However, the most compelling reason why a new U.S. Atlantic initiative is unlikely in the near future may not be the loyalty to the Grand Design of 1962-63. U.S. participation in any free trade area would represent a degree of commitment to integration in the world economy which would require a major political campaign within the United States. Even the passing of the Trade Expansion Act of 1962 demanded dedicated and forceful leadership, and although the full scope of tariff reduction originally permitted by that Act was not far short in economic implications of a cumulative industrial free trade area of the kind described in the Canadian-American Committee Statement of June, 1966, the commitment in the statement is much clearer and, since it would involve treaty arrangements, would appear to political opponents much less reversible. A great deal would be made of the apparent discrimination in a free trade arrangement, at least in its early stages. While the open-ended character of the proposal is a clear answer to this charge, a great deal of past political argument has been devoted to rallying support for the most-favoured-nation multilateralism, and much time and effort might be needed to convince some Americans that regional free trade groupings can be an effective means to the achievement of multilateral ends.

It is difficult to imagine that U.S. industry as a whole would find it difficult to adjust to the challenges of a free trade area. One of the advantages of such a comprehensive scheme is that the complaints of individual firms or sectors of industry need not have so great an importance; the pressure for exceptions can be more effectively resisted, especially if adjustment-assistance provisions such as those incorporated in the Trade Expansion Act of 1962 are included in the treaty. However, traditional protectionism dies hard even in the world's greatest industrial power, and it must not be forgotten that the motives to abandon protection are not likely in the near future to appear as compelling as they were in the Europe of the 1950s.

Nevertheless, if the United States were to decide that a comprehensive free trade arrangement involving the industrially advanced countries would constitute a strong foundation for effective joint action, particularly in aid and trade policy toward the developing countries, then Canada should not be found silent on the sidelines.

OPTION 3: A NORTH AMERICAN FREE TRADE AREA

If Canada's domestic economic and political needs call for a new commercial-policy move, it would appear to be in Canada's own interest as well as that of the Atlantic and developing world first to urge upon the United States a larger initiative. However, if U.S. adoption of such an initiative is improbable, Canada must be prepared to fall back on alternative strategies. Of these the most obvious is a Canada-U.S. free trade area. This has been talked about for many years. In a very limited way the reciprocity arrangement of the mid-nineteenth century is a precedent. But the nature of Canada and of the Canadian economy today is so vastly different that past efforts at reciprocity are scarcely relevant.

What is germane is the fact that the United States regards the Canada-U.S. relationship in a special light. Therefore, if Canada were to fail in its efforts to promote a free trade area embodying Britain and other countries and were to fall back on a Canada-U.S. arrangement or a Western Hemisphere arrangement, the United States would be likely to consider this in an entirely different context from any arrangement extending beyond this hemisphere. Such an arrangement might afford the United States an opportunity to keep alive its efforts in this area, to experiment with the new approach, and to satisfy Canada's economic needs if Canada so interprets them.

So far as Canada is concerned, the key question is whether Canada wishes to contemplate a free trade area in which only Canada and the United States are fully reciprocating members. The answer depends on several considerations—the economic impact on Canadian industry, the constraints imposed on Canadian government economic policy, and the implication for Canada's political interests, internationally and domestically. The economic impact on Canadian industry and the economy generally of a Canada-U.S. free trade area would of course resemble very closely the effects of Canadian participation in any broader association. The industry and regional studies of the Atlantic Economic Studies Program will provide further evidence on this question. However, as suggested earlier, there have been numerous indications that Canadian industries should be able to compete with those of the United States provided that appropriate transitional arrangements are involved.[9]

The effect of free trade on other economic policies is also being examined in those studies in the Atlantic Economic Studies Program which are devoted to policy-harmonization issues. It is clear from European experience that the removal of trade barriers is but a first step in the integration of the economies of independent countries and that the later steps do not follow automatically. Among other policies—customs practices, transportation policies, anti-monopoly regulations, control of capital movements, labour-market policies, stabilization policies, and social services—all may affect, or be affected by, the consequences of the removal of trade barriers. Much will depend on the extent to which the governments of the countries involved already follow parallel policies and on how strong are the preferences in each country for the maintenance of differing practices. One can observe that policy differences prevail between governments of states or provinces in a federal country as well as between countries. It is sometimes suggested that in a larger free trade area Canadian economic policies would not have to be so closely coordinated as they would in one involving only the United States. This is not self-evident, since American policy in many areas might more closely approximate that of members of the group other than Canada, thus requiring a larger Canadian adjustment under these circumstances.

The more purely political considerations have been referred to already. In the international sphere, Canada is anxious to maintain an independent position in world councils. While it is not obvious that Canadian independence would be undermined by further integration of the Canadian and U.S. economies, especially given the degree of interdependence which already exists, other countries, particularly in the developing world, might tend to regard Canada's position as less distinct from that of the United States if she were to become part of a purely North American trade

[9]It is sometimes stated that free trade would reduce the Canadian population or at least its rate of growth. Of course, the tendency of members of the Canadian labour force to emigrate would depend in large part on the competitive position of Canadian industries. If their position is strong, there should be little or no new emigration. The difference in per capita income between the two countries would be reduced by free trade, and therefore the incentive to emigration reduced. However, the population implications can be better assessed when the studies are complete. It should be noted, of course, that it is not easy to justify policy on the grounds of its population effects unless, as was the case in prewar Italy and Germany, the aims of conventional military power are paramount. Under these circumstances it is easier to justify protection for the purpose of supporting a larger population in a self-sufficient economy at a lower standard of living. Presumably most Canadians would be interested in a high per capita income for twenty-five to thirty million fellow Canadians rather than a lower standard of living for a few millions more.

grouping. Presumably Canada's role at the United Nations and elsewhere would provide this country with an opportunity to continue to demonstrate its independence, though it must be admitted that the principal difficulty in convincing others of this arises out of the fact that Canadians so often find their interests and preferences are closely in line with those of the United States.

In domestic politics, it has often been asserted that it is difficult to run on a platform of approval for Canada-U.S. free trade. A few years back the Groupe des Recherches Sociales of Montreal conducted a nation-wide survey. The respondents showed about two-thirds in favour of economic union, with rather little variation from region to region, while less than a third showed an interest in political union. In October, 1966, the Liberal Party Conference voted overwhelmingly in favour of a motion favouring a North American free trade area (including the Caribbean). Although the most one-sided support for this motion came from the four western and the four eastern provinces, substantial support also came from the centre, and not even the economic nationalists, who favour more Canadian ownership of industry, came out against the free trade resolution. Those who did criticize with greatest vigour did so on the grounds that they preferred a wider free trade grouping rather than a purely North American arrangement.

It is hoped that the Atlantic Economic Studies Program will provide more evidence on the economic issues arising out of the closer integration of Canada in the world or the continental economy. It is most unlikely to provide all the answers. But whatever the outcome, both the opportunities and challenges which face Canada in the next few years and the temper of Canadian business, professional, and public opinion demand a more serious reappraisal of Canada's trade policy than has occurred in half a century.

RELATED PUBLICATIONS BY THE
PRIVATE PLANNING ASSOCIATION OF CANADA

CANADIAN TRADE COMMITTEE PUBLICATIONS

THE WORLD ECONOMY

The World Economy at the Crossroads: A Survey of Current Problems of Money, Trade and Economic Development, by Harry G. Johnson, 1965.
The International Monetary System: Conflict and Reform, by Robert A. Mundell, 1965.
International Commodity Agreements, by William E. Haviland, 1963.

CANADA'S TRADE RELATIONSHIPS

Canada's International Trade: An Analysis of Recent Trends and Patterns, by Bruce Wilkinson, 1968.
Canada's Trade with the Communist Countries of Eastern Europe, by Ian M. Drummond, 1966.
Canada's Role in Britain's Trade, by Edward M. Cape, 1965.
The Common Agricultural Policy of the E.E.C. and Its Implications for Canada's Exports, by Sol Sinclair, 1964.
Canada's Interest in the Trade Problems of Less-Developed Countries, by Grant L. Reuber, 1964.

CANADA'S COMMERCIAL POLICY AND COMPETITIVE POSITION

Prices, Productivity, and Canada's Competitive Position, by N. H. Lithwick, 1967.
Industrial Structure in Canada's International Competitive Position: A Study of the Factors Affecting Economies of Scale and Specialization in Canadian Manufacturing, by H. Edward English, 1964.
Canada's Approach to Trade Negotiations, by L. D. Wilgress, 1963.

CANADIAN-AMERICAN COMMITTEE PUBLICATIONS

CANADA-U.S. ECONOMIC RELATIONS

A New Trade Strategy for Canada and the United States (a Statement by the Committee), 1966.
A Possible Plan for a Canada-U.S. Free Trade Area (a Staff Report), 1965.
Invisible Trade Barriers between Canada and the United States, by Francis Masson and H. Edward English, 1963.
Non-Merchandise Transactions between Canada and the United States, by John W. Popkin, 1963.

INVESTMENT

The Role of International Unionism in Canada, by John H. G. Crispo, 1967.
Capital Flows between Canada and the United States, by Irving Brecher, 1965.
Policies and Practices of United States Subsidiaries in Canada, by John Lindeman and Donald Armstrong, 1961.